THE CREATION OF A MASTERPIECE

*"I created you while I was happy, while I was sad,
with so many incidents, so many details.
And, for me, the whole of you has been transformed into feeling."*

C.P. Cavafy

THE CREATION OF A MASTERPIECE

PHOTOGRAPHY:

PETER NEUMANN

TEXT:

JACK A. SOMER

FOUNDATION BOOK JULIET

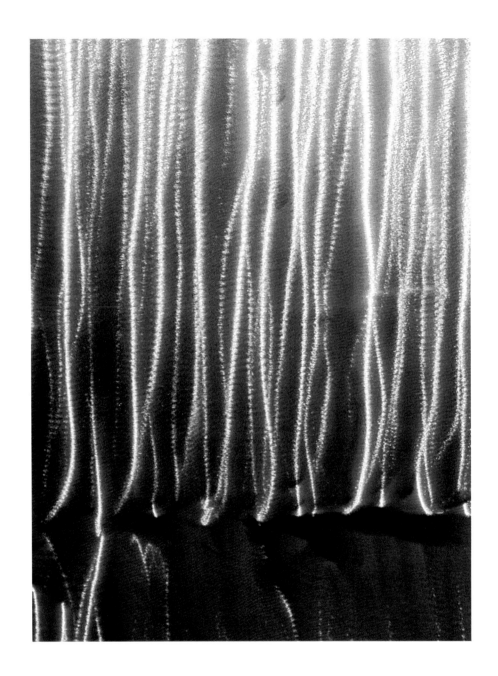

"If you can dream it, we can build it."

———

Wolter Huisman

"My dream is your nightmare."

—

The Client

Juliet
The Creation of a Masterpiece
ISBN 3-88412-172-3

© First published 1993 in Holland by the Foundation Book Juliet
© Copyright 1993 by: Foundation Book Juliet
                         Postbus 23
                         8325 ZG Vollenhove
                         Holland

Layout/Design: Peter Neumann, Jack A. Somer
Typography: YPS Hamburg
Colour reproduction: The Owen Agency
Produced in Great Britain by The Owen Agency

Photo Credits:
Theo Kampa: 21 (1)
Huisman Family: 28 (3)
Jack A. Somer: 150 (1)
Michael Eudenbach: 170 (1)
Dirk Peemöller: Back flap (1)

CONTENTS

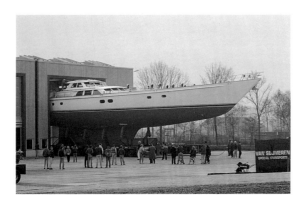

THE TRADITION

"Where the spirit does not work with the hand there is no art." – Leonardo da Vinci

In the year 532, Anthemius of Tralles, a brilliant Greek engineer/architect, was commissioned by Emperor Justinian to replace a church burned down in a terrible rebellion. Eager to finish it, Justinian gave Anthemius 100 overseers and 10,000 laborers and came to the site daily to drive them on, and in five years, ten months and four days the church was completed. Covering 7,564 square meters and topped by a most audacious dome, it was the largest Christian church ever built – *Hagia Sophia*.

In a contract dated 16 August 1501, Michelangelo di Lodovico Buonarroti was commissioned by the Operai of the Cathedral of Florence to create a sculpture. With 400 ducats payment and a time limit of two years, the young Tuscan attacked the project with sharp chisels, obsessive concentration and inspiration from the Greeks, carving deeper and deeper into a colossal block of crystalline marble until all that remained – *three* years later – was his towering monument to human grace and power: *David*.

In 1642 – when it was popular for Dutch business and civic groups to have their portraits painted – Rembrandt Harmensz van Rijn was commissioned by Captain Frans Banning Cocq to portray his Amsterdam militia company – ruffled, feathered and sworded – in a sort of king-size "snapshot." With his earthy palette, masterful *chiaroscuro*, fine brushes and more than a touch of caprice, Rembrandt developed that snapshot into a canvas so grand he elevated a pedestrian assignment into an overwhelming, dynamic work: *The Night Watch*.

In the summer of 1791, his final mortal year, Wolfgang Amadeus Mozart had just completed *The Magic Flute* when he was handed 100 ducats to compose a memorial work by a patron so aloof he sent a surrogate. Though the *who* and *why* of this momentous commission was shrouded in paradox for 173 years – in 1964 it was revealed that the mysterious commissioner, Count von Walsegg, intended to claim the work as his own – the intrigue has never tarnished the divine impulse that gave us Mozart's undisputed masterpiece: *The Requiem*.

And in 1889, calloused iron-mongers completed a dark, uniquely arching structure so new in concept that they barely met the commissioned deadline for the opening of the Centennial of the French Revolution. Engineered and built meticulously to consider wind, weight and the critical eyes of acerbic Parisians, the controversial 300-meter *Eiffel Tower* confirmed mankind's increasing ability to reach heavenward through visionary architecture, sound mathematics and iron.

History and society are enriched by many such wondrous works of art, design and invention, all products of soaring vision and down-to-earth craft. It is no coincidence, then, that they have so many similar threads running through them: For one, each begins from *nothing* – nothing, that is, but unformed raw materials such as amorphous marble, empty canvas or wagon-loads of iron. Second, the inexplicable human forces of insight, enterprise and intellect are harnessed to convert those passive materials into inspiring, everlasting works. Third, each of these works is brought to fruition by the skill and dedication of laborers, craftsmen or artists using ingenious methods and specialized tools – such as Eiffel's prodigious pile-driver or Mozart's frail quill pen – designed to give palpable expression to the ethereal creative urge.

Above all, each of these projects came to fruition only because it was *commissioned*: initiated by a highly focused, severely budgeted, rigidly time-constrained contract between a demanding patron and an eager professional. For, whatever we may think of the abstraction we call "creativity," it almost always does its best work when awakened, impelled and, yes, *paid for* by an enlightened, critical, often stubborn, always uncompromising client. Today, alas, we find fewer such singular commissions: A new minimalist artistic equation is in effect that all but precludes the birth of a more moving *Requiem* or a darker *Night Watch*. And a new economic equation is in effect that forces builders of towers of world trade to abandon the grace of wrought iron, the warmth of hand-carved stone and the breeziness of the French window in favor of steel, concrete and the hopelessly sealed glass wall.

Yet there remain a few patrons who willingly turn their energies, imaginations and no small part of their fortunes to one of humankind's last grand commissions: *the private sailing yacht*. As with yesterday's masterpieces, the making of a modern yacht is an intense synergy between art and science, between heart and hand: It is a striking harmony

◄ *Art and science: a power winch.*

▲ Juliet, *off the Isle of Wight, on her way to sailing the world.*

between rough sketches on foolscap and crisp printouts on Mylar; a translation of vague mental conception into hard-edged lofting; a focusing of diffuse artistry into plasma-sharp cutting; the landing of euphoric flights of imagination by a microchip's swift calculation.

That is why yacht designers are called naval *architects*. Like designers of buildings, they are hired to interpret an often vague notion and intelligently convert it to a new, ideal structure to meet a client's needs. Each time they put pencil to paper, then, both terrestrial and naval architects are expected to produce admirable, solid, long-lasting, self-sustaining environments equipped with humane comforts, essential consumables, reliable machinery, safety devices and proper space for occupants to work, sleep, take meals, use the toilet, convene or be alone. The difference with a sailing yacht, of course, is that it must also float, with grace and

rectitude, and perform according to its "numbers," while it travels the earth's waters unimpeded by the exigencies of weather, the shortage of water, the absence of repair shops, the distance to the office and the dearth of Chinese home-delivery.

The architect Le Corbusier once said that "a house is a machine for living in." Make that a "floating machine" and the definition fits a yacht exquisitely. A modern bluewater sailing yacht is indeed a machine, whose countless parts must function smoothly, predictably, unobtrusively. Its many devices and appliances must work so well, in fact, as to set up no barrier to the thrill of life under sail, whether beneath a shoal of glittering Equatorial stars or amid the melancholy clouds and gray-green seas of a Gulf Stream gale. And a sailing yacht must also function within the corrosive, often destructive environment of the sea: it must be strong yet resil-

▲ The deckhouse, part of a machine for living.

ient, resisting beyond question the threat of massive breaking waves, tiny marine creatures, forbidding coral reefs, harsh sunlight and the occasional spilled Grand Cru. Yet, though it is a machine, a yacht must also disguise its "machineness" in every way, never acknowledging that it is anything but a work of art, a means of passage and a source of bliss.

And, as with *David* or the *Eiffel Tower*, every fine yacht begins as *nothing* – nothing, that is, but stockpiles of raw materials, in storerooms of countless supplying companies, including metals, cables, fabrics, marble, logs, pipes, engines, pumps, appliances, furnishings and fittings. As they lay on their stockroom shelves, these items have no purpose on earth, no value whatsoever, until somewhere in a design office a drawing is approved with their name on it. So it is truly the greatest of marvels that a fine yacht can be erected from so many parts, from so many sources and in so many interwoven processes, and still operate properly, if at all. This marvel, of course, can come to pass only within the infrastructure of a well-organized, well-equipped shipyard. But nothing gets built by shipyards; yachts are built by hard-working, dedicated people expending countless human-hours of time and craft. In the end, it is only acute human minds, skilled human hands and the sweat of a good day's labor that make a yacht real and, with consummate care by all concerned, breathtaking.

Finally, every fine yacht begins with a *commission*, from one dynamic individual who loves the sea: A person who is energized by the process of forging something grand out of *nothing*, then sailing it away. This collaboration consumes many kilowatts of human energy. This book is an attempt to tell the story of one such high-energy collaboration (though in a sense it is also about the processes common to all grand projects). It is the story of *Juliet*, an oceangoing 43.58-meter (142.99-foot) ketch, launched in April 1993. *Juliet* was co-designed by two richly talented men, Ron Holland and Pieter Beeldsnijder. She was built by more than 150 workers of the Royal Huisman Shipyard, in Vollenhove, Holland, under the direction of its principal owner and guiding light, Wolter Huisman. She was assembled from innumerable parts, supplied by hundreds of manufacturers from all over the world. And she was conceived, commissioned and, yes, *paid for* by a 20th-Century client whose enlightened demands and uncompromising expectations patterned the tapestry of her existence. This book is the story of that man as well – the standards he set for himself and which he imposed on others. And though he chooses anonymity here, a not unusual 20th-Century phenomenon, his involvement in every step in his yacht's conception, gestation and birth are undeniable. That involvement will be found carved, subtly or in sharp relief, into every page that follows. So, clearly, will the efforts of the workers of the Royal Huisman Shipyard, to whom we dedicate this book.

▲ *The pilothouse: It also began as nothing.*

THE CONCEPTION

"Nothing contributes so much to tranquilize the mind as a steady purpose –
a point on which the soul may fix its intellectual eye." – Mary Shelley ("Frankenstein")

The gestation of *Juliet* consumed her owner for more than twenty years – an unusual length of time, yes, but certainly not for realizing a life-long dream that began with a simple premise: "to earn some money, buy a boat, and go sailing." You can also be certain that during those twenty years he had other things on his mind and in his briefcase, because he was primarily occupied in redesigning a third-generation family business from a domestic manufacturer into a global marketer. His hard-earned success, and the subsequent sale of the company to a large conglomerate, gave him the freedom to make many new personal choices, one of which was to build a new, very personal yacht.

Twenty years is a long time for any man to ruminate about anything: It requires a magnificent perseverance and it can ignite many explosive impulses – not least of which is the occasional impulse to scrap the whole damned idea and take up the tea ceremony. Because, during the realization of so large a project, even the least vulnerable of men will wake up sharply from many unattainable dreams, face many dismaying crossroads and crumple many rejected sketches along the tortuous path to perfection. Yet if anything can be said of *Juliet*'s owner, it is that he is a perfectionist. His inventiveness is obsessive. He draws upon the ideas of others, to be certain he misses no alternative, then arrives at a solution only after distilling, weighing and discarding each less-than-ideal alternative. And this is a lifelong reflex: He recalls his early years being filled with the intelligent child's curiosity about how everything on earth operates and how everything in the cosmos moves; and at university he studied high-energy physics and engineering, a field with little tolerance for stupidity or inexactitude.

But a perfectionist's attention to detail, no matter how obsessively marshalled, does not alone merit a beautiful boat or a satisfied owner. There are deeper questions relating to the creation of a large, expensive yacht that every thoughtful man must face, even if he can't answer them all to his or the world's satisfaction. First, in this age of overpopulation, forest depletion and threatened ozone, there are environmental concerns. The wind may be free, but a large yacht costs much more than the sum of bills marked "Paid In Full"; it is also accountable to the entire planet in its absorption of raw materials, consumption of energy and creation of waste. While no man would pretend that by constructing a 43-meter yacht he could save one blue whale or defended one puffin

from extinction, the impact of that construction must be minimized, if possible, by a man of conscience.

Second, there are equally sharp questions concerning finance, engineering and practical sailing possibilities: How large can a yacht be before she exceeds the limits of pleasurable handling? How close to the edge can she push sailmaking technology, rigging science and strength of materials? Within how many sweet harbors will she be out of proportion, and how many more shallow bays will deny her entry entirely? How much length can she have to meet aesthetic and spatial demands before bulk overburdens operating costs and exhausts a crew? How massive can she get before

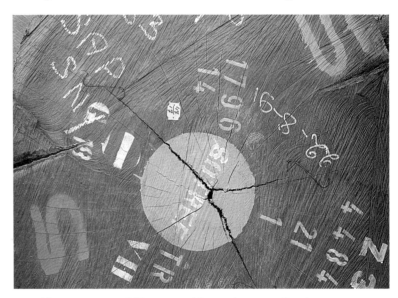

▲ *The process: an old log....* ▼ *The product: new furniture.*

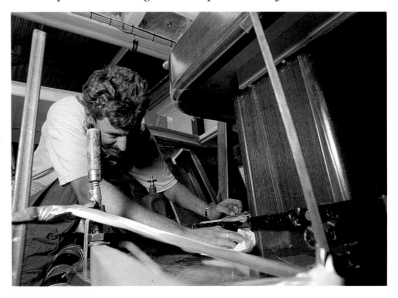

steering her in pressing weather, even with the mechanical advantage of tomorrow's infallible machinery, borders on unsafe? If these questions go unanswered, there are frustrations ahead.

Third, confronting a three-to-five-year design and construction span, a reflective owner must be certain that his desire to build is based upon a solid foundation: an honest passion to go sailing, not a megalomaniac urge to build monuments. Because the heady ferment of the process – with its heated design-room colloquies, vigorous dinner debates, overseas telephone calls, multi-page faxes, sudden inspirations and their costly change orders – can be so obsessive as to completely overwhelm the ultimate objectives of owning a yacht: breathing the sea air, trimming sail to a Tradewind reach and making a landfall in Paradise.

This clash between today's molten desire and tomorrow's chill reality is common. Many creative people are concerned more with *process* than *product*. For them, the venture of building something important is so absorbing that its completion is a letdown, an anticlimax that brings on a form of postpartum depression – what Nietzsche named "The melancholia of everything completed!" For such owners the building process has an aspect of near drug-like dependency, so that when the boat is finally launched they go "cold turkey," suffering symptoms that, ironically, even a long sea voyage won't cure. That is one reason why, in the tight little megayacht society, some gleaming new boats are listed by the brokerage houses within the year their keels are first wetted. Thus, every owner must also ask himself the question: "Can I ever love sailing this creature in a cool ocean breeze as I loved shaping her in an overheated design room?"

Aware of this – one year before *Juliet*'s launch, with the pressure to complete her mounting and a little of that classic anxiety rising – her owner expressed his own private insight into the matter this way: "You must keep going forward in the creative process. If I didn't have this project for the past four years I don't know what I would have done; it would have been a big hole in my life. I will feel sorry when the boat is finished. I am really going to miss coming here [to the Royal Huisman Shipyard]."

Having a nice place to visit and filling a hole in one's life may not, to an outsider, seem compelling enough reasons to spend millions to build a private dream. Yet in his many visits to the yard, numbering about sixty over five years, the owner drew many people into that dream, stretching the talents of every manager and the skills of every craftsman, beyond even their own expectations. So when you watch such an unconventional entrepreneur committing so much of himself and drawing so many dedicated people to him, it is easy to see how a void is filled and how an attachment grows, even as the job gets done. (To stave off leaving Vollenhove, in fact, the owner, over a coffee or perhaps a drink, once offered Wolter

Huisman a trade: *Juliet* for the shipyard. Negotiations stalemated and were broken off when he insisted quite emphatically that Wolter's wife, Ali, was wholly inseparable from the yard.) Now, he has left Vollenhove, and with the world as his home port, he is sharing his creation with good friends, making her an important addition to the annals of yachting.

· ● ·

No one is certain just when yachting became a rationale for sailing, in addition to exploring, war, commerce and fish. Some credit the Egyptians, who dispatched dead Pharaohs to their eternal rest in great craft of wood and gold. Some point to the Phoenicians, who got hooked on boat speed for boat speed's sake, or the Greeks who, between battles with the Persians, rowed their swift triremes around the Aegean just to maintain a good tan. It could have been the South Pacific islanders, who still drift blithely over ocean swells for the fish and the fun of it. The upstart Americans of course have been accused of sailing for hedonism's sake, and even the reserved English have been known to find secret pleasure under sail.

▲ *America's favorite,* Ticonderoga. ▼ *The famed schooner,* Adix.

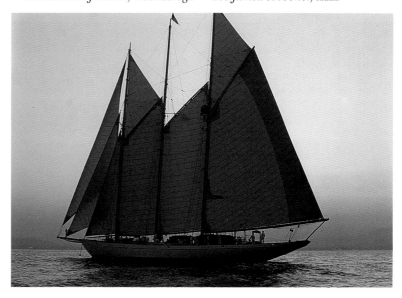

Many historians prefer, however, to blame the Dutch for turning wind-driven vehicles of war or commerce into sources of escape, largely by their genius in creating craft that, as Hans Vandersmissen described in a pamphlet, "look like clogs but sail like devils." It was coincidentally the Dutchman Adrian Block who, in 1613, built the first *jaght schip* in America, *Onrust*. The *jaght schip* – though it gave us the word "yacht" – was not strictly a pleasure craft, but a typically light and fast boat suitable for many purposes. Block sailed *Onrust* around Nieuw Amsterdam's waters long before the World Trade Center cast its wind shadow, so he knew the full joy of a day on the water, and many smart sailors followed him.

The man who broke the modern pleasure barrier, in 1816, was George Crowninshield, who built a 25-meter hermaphrodite brig he named *Cleopatra's Barge*. Her incomparable mahogany, birds-eye maple and red velvet furniture, gilt fixtures, gold lace, mirrors, chandelier, custom-made china and glass set a standard of luxury unknown to that time (and not too common in *this*). Painted as gaudily as today's spinnakers, with herringbone stripes on one side and horizontals on the other, she may not have been to everybody's taste, but she no doubt inspired generations of the wealthy to create floating palaces: Whether decorated serenely with white-painted wood and varnish, or built as ornate, panelled treasuries for antiques and collected art, yachts such as *Valhalla*, *Atlantic*, *Ticonderoga*, *Adix*, *Orion* and *Shenandoah* are masterpieces that serve their masters well.

Surely, if any yacht stands as the ultimate masterpiece of our time it is the 107.5-meter, four-masted barque *Sea Cloud*. Built as *Hussar* in 1931 by Krupp/Germania in Kiel, and painted black, she was a rather generous, if forbidding, wedding present for Marjorie Merriweather Post from her husband Edward F. Hutton (to whom "everybody listened" until junk bonds silenced his progeny). *Sea Cloud* survived the Hutton's divorce, two more Post marriages, service in Leningrad, World War II submarine hunting, sale to a Dominican dictator, renaming to *Angelita*, *Patria*, *Atarna* and back to *Sea Cloud*, and repainting to white. Her hull and rig are throwbacks, her interior implies royalty.

But after her heyday, the 20th Century began to witness changes, and *Sea Cloud* now serves less exclusive purposes. At the same time, steam railways, slow ships and grand touring cars were supplanted by *maglev* trains, SSTs and Ferraris. Today we willingly forego a leisurely walk to buy the newspaper in favor of jumping into the family auto; factories run by computers and robots crank out a world of artless product, and the demands of earning a fortune, or scratching out a mere living, consume nearly all our leisure time. We must therefore take courage from those rare individuals who still desire, still have the time, and can still afford to voyage freely over the horizon, seeking discovery, surprise and freedom, under a cloud of sail, on the deck of a yacht that is an expression of themselves.

Perhaps this wondrous sociohistoric circumstance was best predicted in 1691 by the Englishman Sir Dudley North. North was the quintessential entrepreneur of his day. He was a driven man who amassed a fortune through mastery of intricate Turkish business dealings (no mean feat for an Englishman) and who wrote a definitive treatise on trade that preceded the better-known work of Adam Smith. We borrow his prophetic words indirectly from Jon Bannenberg, the noted yacht designer and stylist who quoted North appropriately in his own 1987 personal testament of design strategy and social science, *YACHTS*:

[T]he main spur to Trade, or rather to Industry and Ingenuity, is the exorbitant Appetites of Men, which they will take pains to gratifie, and so be disposed to work, when nothing else will incline them to it; for did Men content themselves with bare Necessaries, we should have a poor World.

▲ *The barque* Sea Cloud: *regal below* … ▼ *royal under sail.*

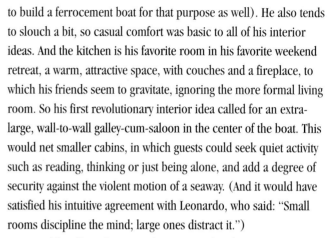

*"Man does not conquer the sea simply by buying a boat.
He must create for himself a new design for living."* – Boris Lauer-Leonardi

Like many modern men, *Juliet*'s owner is intrigued by technology, fascinated by computers and attracted to the machine power of contemporary sailing yachts. Yet he has an eye for the art and the majesty of a classic yacht as well. He started sailing at six, and as a lad he messed around, with friends, in small boats along the New England coast. He likes the Boothbay Challenger, a famous American design. He sailed his own Hinckley 41 for years. He admires Philip Rhodes's many masculine, seaworthy motorsailers. He thinks the "Wizard of Bristol," Nathanael Herreshoff, did no wrong (in that notion, he is surely not alone). He is not interested in racing. Not at all. After a Caribbean charter in the early 1980s on a 65-foot Swan that he found entirely pleasurable, he began thinking of someday owning a similar craft. But he wanted just "a bit more boat," so he tucked in the back of his mind the notion of a "stretch" version, with perhaps ten feet added to assure more living space and better crew quarters, as he believes in the valid old maxim about happy crews equating to happy boats.

He also sought features that he found wanting in many other designs. He wanted easy steering, not the bestial sort found on purebred offshore racers that would take the fun out of sailing and deny his occasional urge to handle her alone (one of the sailing life's prime visceral thrills). He wanted a yacht so brimming with technical reliability and shaped in such a timeless style that in 30 years she would neither be mechanically nor aesthetically outdated, even as other yachts inevitably would. Therefore he wanted a yacht of handsome appearance, one that was "trim and balanced but not extreme in any way." He wanted, in short, what we would glibly call a "modern classic": the easiest thing on earth to ask for, surely the most difficult to acquire.

As with many yachts, *Juliet*'s design grew largely out of her interior conception, for which the client had a deluge of original ideas. He disdains formality, having spent many youthful bohemian days and communal nights roaming with pals in a caravan equipped with a hibachi grill, a roof sundeck and a guitar, in search of independence (he once tried

Escaping the sun.... ▶

to build a ferrocement boat for that purpose as well). He also tends to slouch a bit, so casual comfort was basic to all of his interior ideas. And the kitchen is his favorite room in his favorite weekend retreat, a warm, attractive space, with couches and a fireplace, to which his friends seem to gravitate, ignoring the more formal living room. So his first revolutionary interior idea called for an extra-large, wall-to-wall galley-cum-saloon in the center of the boat. This would net smaller cabins, in which guests could seek quiet activity such as reading, thinking or just being alone, and add a degree of security against the violent motion of a seaway. (And it would have satisfied his intuitive agreement with Leonardo, who said: "Small rooms discipline the mind; large ones distract it.")

The client also wanted assurance that those cozy spaces were acoustically isolated and perfectly private: You can't build a floating pleasure dome and then crawl into a bunk from which you hear generators, pumps, compressors, anchor-chains, music, toilets, conversation and other intimacies. And, in the interests of further assuring his tranquility, and in respect for the environment, he wanted a "battery boat," one that would rely on great banks of stored electric potential and minimal generator power, to save fuel and allow him long periods of silence at anchor and under sail, fundamental blessings of the cruising life.

And this man, a young man, enjoys lounging playfully and entertaining large groups of friends, so he sought a broad foredeck that provides open spaces for wandering about, and an equally broad afterdeck with corners for tucking in and sleeping under the stars, without cleats or blocks digging into his back. And he wanted space to stow and easily deploy all manner of motorized and sailing dinghies and countless water toys for the pleasure of his guests. Also, he wanted those guests to have an easy choice between enjoying the sun's warmth or escaping its dangers, but never at the sacrifice of a fresh breeze in their faces or a good view of the sea, so the design of an enclosed deckhouse and an open pilothouse became critical issues throughout the design process. He also wanted a choice of sociably oriented steering stations, each with a good view of the sea and the sailplan, each within easy somehow to get the builder of his dream yacht to devise a unique elevating crow's nest that would ride high on the mainmast, and from which a lookout might pick out dangerous coral heads rimming a Pacific atoll, or where he and no more than one intimate friend might view the world and operate the boat in solitude and silence, just in case deck-level social pressures encroached unbearably upon them.

As a man committed to business and the microchip, he wanted to carry a variety of computers, global telephones, telex, facsimile, audio and video gear and lots of music in the form of compact discs, electronic and acoustic instruments for those communal evenings reminiscent of the days when the sound of guitars and bongos bound him to his buddies. And finally, he visualized an interior with an original furniture styling that was also fresh and timeless: that referred to the past but had elements of more modern thinking, again in the "modern classic" vein. This would normally be a perplexing challenge to a stylist or architect; such demands are made every day by clients who don't know what they want (except that they don't want to lose much of their investment when it comes time to sell). But in this case it came from a man with a strong feeling for design, and a secure knowledge of his universe. Some of these wonderful ideas, of course, were more noble fantasies than tenable solutions. *Juliet*'s interior plan evolved more conventionally, though with so much original detail it can hardly be deemed conventional. And despite the owner's environmental concerns and the shipyard's will to make a "battery boat," *Juliet* grew into a pushbutton sailing craft laden with so many power consumers that she developed inexorably into a "generator boat."

Surely, the greatest single issue in *Juliet*'s design was arriving at her final length. She started, in 1984, as a "stretch 65." But she expanded within a few years, because in France the client discovered *Ebb Tide*, a well-cut 85-foot Sparkman & Stephens gem built by the Royal Huisman Shipyard. He was, as he recalls, "stunned by her, she was so huge and powerful!" He was so smitten, in fact, that he bought her, had her original interior designer, Pieter Beeldsnijder, modify her, and he took off sailing to help his new boat jell in his mind. *Ebb Tide*, in fact, became his sort of "training ship" for what was by now a 90-foot design, and he set a rough mental budget of $3.5 million dollars on the project. But, as such things happen, once he was immersed in the planning of his new boat, he came to admire yet another one: Noel Lister's *Whirlwind XII*, a 103-foot Ron Holland ketch also built by the Huisman yard, whose superb cruising qualities became his new, more focused mental target. As we will see later, in just one more year, and for countless alluring reasons, the target grew another forty feet.

▲ Juliet, *on a close reach off Nantucket.*

"I HAVE AN IDEA ..."

"The bottom line is in heaven." – Edwin H. Land

Whirlwind XII was not yet two years old in the spring of 1988 when, in the good company of an old friend, but without a design or designer in mind, the client toured Europe in search of a builder. Europe, with its age-old tradition of craftsmanship and its ancient connection to the sea, is a cornucopia of illustrious shipyards: from Finland to Italy, from Spain to Denmark, from Britain to Germany, from Greece to France, there are yards capable of superb construction, systems and finish, the main elements of a superior yacht. Each yard's management is ready to offer a cup of coffee, a tour of the facilities and reasons to build with them; each yard leaves a distinct sensual impression, whether the clangor of steel, the fragrance of resin, the glint of alloy welding or the drifting dust of wood.

Yet, after visiting some coolly efficient yards of the north and warmly chaotic yards of the south, when the client reached the Royal Huisman Shipyard, standing starkly along a narrow grass-lined canal in the Dutch village of Vollenhove, his search came to an end. He was already aware of Huisman's reputation for quality – two of his favorite boats, *Ebb Tide* and *Whirlwind*, were built there – and he was impressed by the clean, organized offices and design rooms. But these appearances could be found elsewhere. What truly stopped him was seeing the yard's workers: Even through a barrier of language he found them exuberant, animated, concerned. He was simply touched by the atmosphere, convinced that this was a happy place to build a yacht. "I fell in love with the place," he recalls. "Wolter Huisman is the Santa Claus of yachting and his yard is Santa's workshop. I said to myself: *This is where I want to build a boat*."

A happy place? Falling in love? Santa's workshop? Surely these are trivial, childish or, worse, mistaken reasons for selecting a shipyard's hard-headed technicians, scorched welders, skilled machinists, crafty woodworkers and speckled painters to build you a large, expensive boat. What could a welder's humor have to do with the solidity of his welds, or an electrician's temper with his wiring? The answer is: *Everything*. For a sensitive client to hand over to a shipyard the mission of creating a multi-million dollar yacht, he *must* have such feelings. In an age of

assembly-line existence, we forget that good quality is a human achievement. Choosing a shipyard can indeed be influenced by glimpsing workers, tape measures and tools in hand but without a manager haranguing them, gather to solve a small problem.

That attitude, of course, comes from the top. This becomes apparent when a visit to the Huisman yard begins at the flower-encircled Huisman bungalow, where a pleasant Dutch-style luncheon is served by Ali Huisman, a demanding member of the yard's advisory board as well as Wolter Huisman's wife. The luncheon is filled with good cheer, good cheese and good banter about politics, economics or the weather (as in Indianapolis, if you don't like it, wait a minute). The view from the dining room embraces the flat grassy countryside, dotted with cows and geese, framed by distant trees, backed by bold cumulus clouds and permeated by flowing water, too flat and open perhaps to be pure Ruysdael or Hobbema, yet typically Dutch. So long as a guest joins freely in the spirituality of grace before and after the meal, accepts the drooling affections of a big Newfoundland pup and can make sense of an inverted Dutch barometer that "rises" when it "falls," life in the Huisman corner of Vollenhove is both blessed and agreeable and, yes, a happy place to build a boat.

Within two days of his arrival, the client signed a routine letter of intent to build a 105-foot yacht (*Juliet* had already grown in *Whirlwind*'s shadow). "No one had ever ordered a boat that quickly," he recalls, with a certain twinkle in his eye. But as the ink dried, the letter of intent already faced obsolescence, as another masterpiece was under construction in the shed next to Wolter Huisman's office. There are two doors to that office: one opens on a long office-lined corridor; the other opens on a precipitous spiral staircase (like the terrorizing one inside the Statue of Liberty). Opening that door, one is immediately faced with the project farthest along in the Huisman schedule. In the spring of 1988 that project happened to be the 140-foot *Cyclos III. Cyclos* – designed for grace and speed by Ron Holland, with an immaculate interior by Andrew Winch – was the Huisman's largest and, with *Acharné*, its most complex build to

◀ *ING Bank, Amsterdam*

date. Yet for all her trim, shipshape, lacquer and leather coolness, *Cyclos* was to play a seminal role in the birth of *Juliet*, one of the warmest yachts ever built.

• • •

Some months (and some meetings) after the signing, the yard presented the client with a heavy, official-looking, spiral-bound 83-page book entitled "Contract Specification Yard No. 357A" (the Huisman yard's modern numbering system began at 200, so *Juliet* is the 157th aluminum yacht). The book, a standard Huisman practice and prepared under the careful guidance of commercial director Evert van Dishoeck, outlined technical parameters for the build of a 105-foot (32-meter) ketch with time-tables for each stage in the design, construction and delivery. Later the book would be rewritten several times as *Juliet* grew until, more than a year later, her length was fixed at 43.58 meters and a firm price was quoted by the yard. While it is not appropriate here to discuss that price – you may safely assume that *Juliet* was *not* inexpensive – this is a good moment to see how the yard normally quotes its prices.

Calculating the cost of a 43-meter yacht is not easy: There are thousands of inventory parts and thousands of worker hours to be accounted for, which is more than a matter of careful arithmetic; it must be accomplished in a controlled business environment. During any project, for example, the yard issues biweekly statements covering the financial aspects of the work; to develop confidence in the process, however, the client is welcome at any time to see the raw data from which the statements are derived. As further assurance, representatives from the Zwolle office of the international accounting firm of Coopers & Lybrand perform regular checks of account reports so clients know that an independent auditor stands behind the numbers. Of equal importance, Coopers & Lybrand also provides auditing and tax consulting services, and assists the yard in obtaining government grants for research and development, which should interest a client almost as much as the bottom line. Also, the yard is insured by the Amsterdam brokerage Rollins Hudig Hall, whose broad-based policy covers infrastructure, machinery, inventory, employees, business interruption, hull transportation and progressive hull value (to indemnify clients against loss during construction) – all up to the delivery of the yacht. And the yard is backed by Internationale Nederlanden Bank (ING Bank.), part of ING Group, one of Europe's major financial institutions. Like most banks,ING tailors corporate services and savors financing distinctive projects. But *unlike* most banks, ING lives in a jostling ten-towered "S"-shaped complex rising from Amsterdam's earth like a Luna Park fun city. But it is not funny; it is a brilliant, robust habitat whose gardens supply herbs to its restaurants, oxygen to the ventilators and refreshment to its depositors.

▲ Ebb Tide, *the initiator.* ▼ Whirlwind XII, *the inspiration.*

▼ Cyclos III, *whose hull lines and rig set the standard for* Juliet.

With all this in the background, there of course comes a time when the yard must actually figure the cost of a project and quote a price. How is it done? Well, in the early 1980s, Wolter Huisman shifted over to the cruising-yacht market after building mostly racing boats. It was a startling shift for him. When a full-blooded racing sailor ordered a boat he was likely to want a light hull, a skinny rig and bunks stuffed with straw to keep his campaign Spartan and fast. By contrast, Wolter soon learned that cruising sailors are, shall we say, somewhat less manageable; they have many more options open to them and they want everything plush, grand and overbuilt. Wolter realized that no project would conclude as it began; every yacht would grow in size and intricacy right up to its launching, and sometimes beyond.

With so much that was unpredictable it became difficult to quote a profitable yet competitive price beforehand. So his financial director, Bert Loof, developed a pricing system the yard has used for most projects since 1984, billing some 160 million Dutch guilders to 1993 (nearly 100 million dollars at 1993 exchange rates). To make its quote, the yard first considers, out of its long accumulated experience, the size of the boat and its equipment needs and establishes the costs for materials, labor and overhead, by category (construction, machinery, systems, interior, electronics, paint etc.). It then adds a fair percentage for its guarantee and profit. Simple. So long as the overall length is set and no extreme changes are made, the *guilder* profit, not the *percentage* profit, is fixed; for reasonable additions, the yard charges only its direct cost. As an example, if a two-generator boat under construction requires a third generator, the client pays only cost on it. The system is honorable. It impels the yard to finish a boat on time and at the projected cost or, if possible, under cost. It also assures a client that the yard has no financial interest in making a project more complex or time-consuming (no yard wants to keep a boat around longer than necessary). Finally, it encourages everyone to mutually search for new technical solutions so that development continues in a healthy, cooperative atmosphere.

Once *Juliet* was under way, the client came to recognize the benefits of this fixed-profit system: "We had no limits," he said. "The important thing was to get it done. Sometimes I'm glad I didn't know the cost of every item, though no single idea was ever thrown out just for cost. Without this system I could never have gotten the boat I wanted." Ron Holland quite agreed when, halfway through the build, he said: "If you get the best boat in the world, who really cares about the price?" And Jens Cornelsen agreed emphatically: "This accounting system

is the only way to get the greatest boat in the world." Cornelsen should know: He soon became the client's contract project manager, playing a critical technical and administrative role in *Juliet*'s coming into being.

It is a given that a project of this magnitude – even with a wise client and a trustworthy shipyard – needs a third party with fresh opinions who, though not necessarily an expert in every field, will work to achieve the client's desires, or explain to the client why they are unattainable. A project manager is a specialist who can sit in on planning meetings as a technical and financial buffer at the client's side, or act as a surrogate in his absence. Cornelsen's basic tasks were to vouch for the yard's building *Juliet* as the client contracted them to do by checking drawings and installations, monitoring costs, seeing to it that no one lost sight of the forest of completion for the numerous trees of change (this client made so many changes, it would have been quite easy to get lost in that forest), and later attending all sea trials as a final check on the yard's work. Though the client visited the yard often, and was always in contact by phone or fax, he still needed Cornelsen to represent him between visits to avoid having to come more often (probably to the yard's great relief).

To qualify for this work Cornelsen studied engineering, apprenticed at MAN diesels, did time in the German navy, sailed in several Admiral's Cups and spent eight years overseeing the build of 15 Swan 65s in the "salt mines" of Pietarsaari, Finland. He has managed dozens of projects to designs by Sparkman & Stephens, Judel & Vrolijk, Bruce King, John Alden, German Frers and the late Henry Scheel. When he's not gallivanting about the yacht yards of the world, Cornelsen works in his studio in Gluckstadt, Germany, a bright space filled with half models, photos and memorabilia from which he does insurance claim work and surveying, and his wife Dorit runs an in-operation yacht management concern, which provides numerous services to yacht owners and their crews. When he has time, he occasionally sails his rebuilt 5.5-Meter.

Cornelsen sees himself as a chemist busy mixing ingredients. "I am the one person who gets all the input among owner, yard, designer and stylist," he says. "I prefer to work with a client who appreciates quality, who initiates the thought process. That is why *Juliet* was so different, so much more complicated in every

respect than any other projects. The client was tough; he challenged everybody for new ideas. It was not unusual for me to receive a call early in the morning from him that began: *I have an idea....*"

◄ *Jens Cornelsen, project manager.*

THE SHIPYARD

"Don't fight forces; use them." – R. Buckminster Fuller

Wolter Huisman was 14 years old in the spring of 1945, as a fresh wind blew the oily smoke of war from Europe's skies, no longer filled with Stukas, Lancasters, ME-109s and B-17s. To immobilize the Dutch, the Nazis had opened floodgates and sluices that held back the sea; 1945 was a time to rebuild an infrastructure as well as a nation. It was also time for Wolter to put on his wooden shoes and go to work in his father's muddy little boatyard in Ronduite, in northwest Overijssel Province in central Holland. Wolter's grandfather had started the yard in 1884, with the tongue-twisting name Overijsselse Jachtwerf W. Huisman BV, to build boats for the transport of cattle and hay along the canals, and for fishermen who made their living from the sea. Now, under Wolter's father Jan, who had taken over in 1928, the yard was building boats for yachtsmen to take their pleasure on that same salty sea.

There were no schools for boatbuilding in 1945, so Jan taught young Wolter carpentry and set him to work on a traditional clinker-built dinghy (not unlike the one that resides in *Juliet*'s lazarette today). With fresh confidence, the mighty Huisman team – Jan, Wolter and just one employee – resumed work on two boats that had been ordered before the war (even then Huisman clients were willing to wait out long delivery schedules in return for good quality). A dozen more wood boats followed. In 1950, Wolter left to serve a 22-month stint in the Dutch Navy, doing some "official" sailing. When he returned home, having had a good taste of the rough North Sea and the rugged steel ships that defy it, he convinced his father that they should abandon wood hulls and turn to building boats of steel. In 1954, they bought bending machines and primitive welding equipment and landed their first orders: a motorboat and two small sailing yachts designed by Van de Stadt and Robert Clark, to whom Wolter still feels a deep debt of gratitude. Over the next few years the team, enlarged to 22 workers, built 30 more steel boats.

But the march of technology spurred on by the post-war recovery was inspiring yacht builders everywhere to search for lighter, more competitive materials. In the early 1960s, with molded fiberglass already revolutionizing small-boat production and threatening to overtake the market,

Since 1971 ... in Vollenhove. ▶

the Huismans joined the competitive fray by attempting to lighten a steel boat with an aluminum superstructure and deck. But they couldn't weld the aluminum very well and, frustrated, used teak instead. Soon Wolter saw a newspaper advertisement for the giant aluminum processor AlCan, showing a Dutch-built all-alloy motorboat; he was intrigued. He contacted the company and they treated him to a tour of that other fledgling boat builder, Strijker (later Striker), in Oss, whose pioneering work in 30- to 40-foot sportboats convinced him of aluminum's enormous, versatile potential.

In 1964, Wolter Huisman closed the door on the crude world of heavy, rusty, smelly steel and commissioned a nine-meter Van de Stadt design, frameless to maximize the interior volume. "We got new equipment and began welding," Wolter recalls. "We welded, welded and welded, but we still didn't get it right. It was terrible; some of the welds looked like bread inside." AlCan again came to the rescue, introducing him to the Metal Inert Gas (MIG) technique, and the yard embarked on a period of building more and more sophisticated racing boats and semi-production yachts. Wolter built – and even raced with his clients on – *Spirit of Delft*, *Noryema*, *Prospect of Whitby*. He produced one-offs including *Saudade*, a German Admiral's Cup winner. And he created a series of Avenirs to Van de Stadt lines, one of which was for an avid Berlin sailor named Herman Noack. Noack's art foundry did much of the bronze casting for the English sculptor Henry Moore; he had an eye for quality that Huisman satisfied, and Noack, who remains a close family friend, has since built four more boats there, all named *Sabina*.

In 1965 the Huisman name took a giant leap across the Atlantic when Rod Stephens of Sparkman & Stephens expressed his faith by ordering a 60-foot sloop – the largest Huisman boat to date – for an American client, Jakob Isbrandtsen. The handsome *Running Tide*, with her 12-Meter profile, open interior and gleaming finish, became a symbol of excellence everywhere she sailed, and initiated a 25-year relationship during which the yard built 35 S&S boats.

By 1971, with his father retired, the local canals too shallow to launch his larger boats and business outgrowing the old yard, Wolter took his wooden shoes out of the Ronduite mud and moved his welding gear, work-

▲ *Wolter Huisman.*

▲ *The Royal Huisman Shipyard.*

▲ *Grandfather Wolter and family, 1905.* ▼ *Wolter's father Jan.*

▼ *Wolter and Ali Huisman in a breeze.*

ers and family ten kilometers down the road to the present site in Vollenhove. By then Ali had given him three daughters, Alice, Caroline and Mirjam (who are all part of the yard's team). He attended evening school to study metal work, welding, drawing and bookkeeping. In the daytime, as "big boss," he worked in the office, sneaking out to the construction floor on occasion "just to help the boys," because, as he says, "office work is not real work; real work is with the hands." He built more illustrious racers such as *Pinta*, *Mandrake* and *Revolution*. In 1975 he started a spar and hardware division, Rondal, a name he coined from the "Rond" of Ronduite and the "al" from aluminum. In 1976 he built Connie van Rietschoten's first *Flyer*, which won the Whitbread Round the World Race. In 1980 he delivered *Helisara VI* to Maestro Herbert von Karajan. Aluminum had matured. Life was good.

But in the early 1980s the shipyard hit a wall: A new level of confusion over offshore racing rules and improved plastics and composites caused the demand for sophisticated aluminum racing boats to slide to a shocking halt. Wolter had 65 people on his staff with virtually no work, yet he refused to lay anyone off. So, after building some of the world's best-known ocean racers, Wolter Huisman turned with conviction to the cruising market, never looking back. "I'm not interested in building racing boats any more," Wolter says today. "We've changed too much. Yes, we made a good success with racing; but cruisers are more complex, more challenging. I enjoy the complexity. It's headaches, yes, but on the other hand it's nice." It is, indeed, a large cruising yacht's "nice headaches" that stretch the talents of the current 150-odd Huisman workers. Most are local folk; few have traveled far, except by bicycle in summer or on skates during a cold winter when Holland's canals freeze hard. Some go to technical schools; few have attended university. There are no PhDs on the staff, and the local joke is that few even know what a PhD is. And though yacht building is in nature an elitist industry, Huisman workers depend upon pride and innate skill, rather than advanced theoretical studies.

Sharing that pride, Wolter Huisman looks back at the unquestioned pinnacle of his working life: a day in 1984, on the yard's 100th anniversary, when Her Majesty Queen Beatrix of the Netherlands bestowed the title *Royal* Huisman Shipyard BV. The "Royal" designation is a singular honor for companies that have achieved recognition in their fields; Huisman was the 120th to be so honored, joining Royal Dutch Airlines, Royal Shell and the Royal Concertgebouw Orchestra. But as Wolter claims, with his usual humility, the award honors his grandfather, father and the tradition they created, not him. And, as he sometimes reminds a visitor, the honor can also be taken away. As you see *Juliet* come to life here, you will know why the odds against that happening are rather high.

• • •

There is a tale told in Holland, the Bible notwithstanding, that Creation took eight days, not seven. It was on the eighth day that the humble people living on the marshes bordering the North Sea reclaimed the Low Countries, with their own hands, from the sea. They built homes and farms and made something marvelous for the future out of the mud. That is, again, just a tale. In truth, Holland's odd geological character took shape at the end of the last Ice Age, when the receding polar ice cap bulldozed its way northward leaving behind a flat coastal plain, much of it beneath sea level, that is, according to Erasmus, "intersected by navigable rivers full of fish and abounding in rich pastures." Holland is still is mostly under sea level – "The hell of Holland is water," is the way the locals see it. Thus, Nature created the Netherlands (the Land Beneath) not so much as a haven for the good life as a roadblock to it. It required energetic human inhabitants thousands of years to wall out the sea, reclaim that marsh and make it prosper. (In *The Embarrassment of Riches*, Simon Schama says: "Dutchness was often equated with the transformation, under divine guidance, of catastrophe into good fortune, infirmity into strength, water into dry land, mud into gold.") Over its history, the area was inhabited by Bronze Age brutes, Roman rulers, early Germanic tribes (Frisians are still there), Carolingians, Norse invaders, the Dukes of Burgundy, the Habsburgs and Emperor Charles the V and his son Philip II, who made it Spanish. The 1579 Union of Utrecht brought a semblance of outline to the land, which won independence in 1648, after the Eighty Years' War with Spain.

By then, the tiny United Provinces had attained enormous wealth and far-reaching sea power through a fleet of 2,700 ships. But the Golden Age of the United East-India Company was soon eclipsed by England and France; Holland receded into a quiet, private, non-colonial abundance. Once the Kingdom of the United Netherlands was proclaimed in 1815 by King William I, the entity officially called the Netherlands, but which most of us warmly call Holland, assumed its place among the nations. Vollenhove is first mentioned in Dutch historic works in the year 944, when it was "put on the map" with the odd name *Fulnaho* by Holy Roman Emperor Otto The Great, who traveled far from his German home to indulge his favorite passion: pig hunting. By 1165 a large Episcopal castle, Het Oldehuus, was completed (its moat was converted to a fishing port in 1823, after the original castle was destroyed). In 1354, the Bishop of Utrecht granted the village municipal rights, the beginning of the Vollenhove's modern history. By the 17th Century Vollenhove was a major Zuyder Zee trading port with a roadstead for a great fishing fleet, so the harbor was breakwatered. But after engineers dammed off the Zuyder Zee in the 1930s, as part of a grand reclamation scheme, the fishing industry scattered and the harbor was converted to a marina. Vollenhove is now the seat of government for the six-town municipality, Gemeente Brederwiede, an area rich in lakes, navigable canals and friendly attractions, administered by a Lord Mayor, who sits in a 600-year-old stone office a few hundred meters from the yard's imposing metal and glass complex. The marina, expanded in 1993, is just across the N-331 road from the yard. But as you will see, it is totally inaccessible to Huisman yachts. Totally.

▲ *The reed-cutters of Ronduite.*

THE DESIGN TEAM

*"No doubt the shape of a yacht or vessel is influenced by so many factors
that the necessary compromises and combinations may be best dealt with by art." – L. Francis Herreshoff*

To most casual observers a sailboat is a graceful hull, cleaving a forgiving sea, with all sail drawing, under fair-weather clouds, in a sultry breeze, granting a carefree life. It is an oil painting by an old master, a vision of beauty in a harsh world. In short, it is pure fantasy. In reality a sailboat is a highly calculated, cautiously structured vehicle designed to give pleasure, but also to survive the nightmare of a violent sea. It is not casually conceived: its shape is the premeditated merging of many visible and invisible elements – entry angle, transom curve, waterline beam, tumblehome, bow angle, keel profile, the rake of the rig and the aspect of the rudder. The distinguishing quality of the best yachts is that these elements generate stable, safe performance while blending into a harmonic whole such that the observer is unaware of the parts. (It is somewhat like watching a perfect racing jibe from afar: One sees only the hull turn smoothly under the spinnaker; never the frantic, sweaty ballet on deck.)

Under normal circumstances, achieving that harmony is difficult enough for a designer. Yet, with *Juliet* there were two factors that complicated the design: First was a client who, though not trained as a naval architect, had compelling preconceptions that could rightfully override any *single* designer's ideas. Second was his choice of *two* accomplished naval architects, each at the peak of a highly competitive career, to collaborate on that design. His decision came from a growing conviction that the boat he dreamed

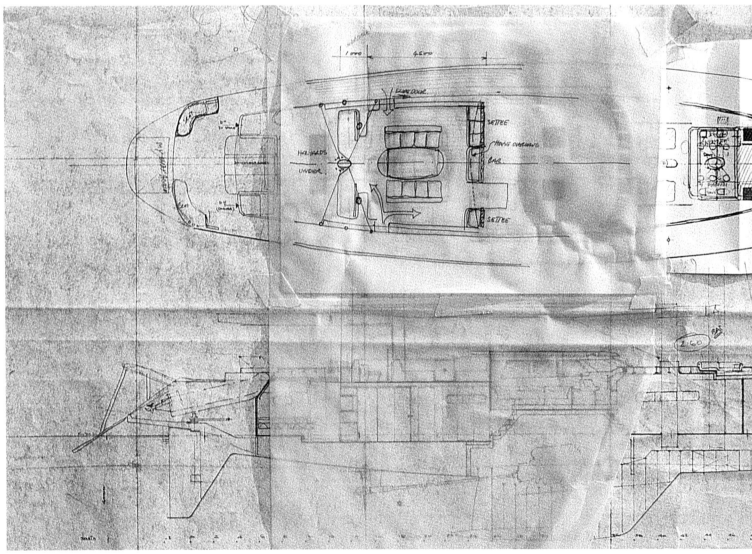

The collaboration: on blueprint, fax and tracing paper. ▲

of during those twenty years was so sophisticated it demanded a collaboration. He chose Ron Holland, a New Zealander living in Ireland, to do the hull and rig because Holland had drawn a series of highly admired cruising yachts over 100 feet, beginning with *Whirlwind XII*, and had learned from and matured with each of his subsequent boats. He chose Pieter Beeldsnijder, a Dutch naval architect living in Edam, to style the yacht because he admired his originality and flair for an overall conception and his versatility (he had designed dozens of sailboats, motoryachts such as *Jefferson Beach*, Falcon aircraft and even Akai stereo equipment). He particularly was pleased by the work Beeldsnijder did on *Ebb Tide*.

Collaboration is not every designer's cup of tea. Yes, Holland and Beeldsnijder had already collaborated on *Happy Joss*, a 75-foot Royal Huisman sloop launched in 1989, but there the division had been sharp: Holland was the technician, Beeldsnijder the stylist. With *Juliet*'s far greater design demands, the division was destined to be blurred, and potentially discordant. One doesn't normally think of yacht design as a *political* process, but it took a few months for the client to negotiate an agreement between the two to accept the shared responsibility, ultimately seeing to it that

▲ *Ron Holland.* ▼ *Pieter Beeldsnijder.*

▼ *Huisman design office.*

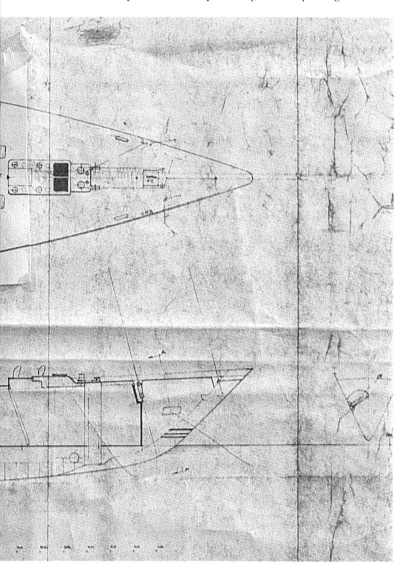

egotism took a back seat. "It was a great accomplishment getting these two talented men together to fiddle with each other's lines," he said. "We were all equals at the table. The camaraderie and love of the project were more important than any one person's ideas. We were looking for solutions, not personal statements. We just wanted it all to work."

And work it did: In the meetings that followed so many ideas were presented, and with such uninhibited intellectual energy, that the identity of any single idea's author was lost, and the notion of a single inventor became an absurdity. Though the client credits Beeldsnijder with the "look" of the boat and Holland for her superb performance, you cannot today see *Juliet* and scribe a line on her that divides a performance-driven idea from an aesthetic one – a true measure of any teamwork. But *Juliet* is more than a Beeldsnijder/Holland work. She was also designed by key Huisman project managers and technicians, using their own practical experience to consummate some of the most important details, long after the basic design was approved.

Still, you might ask just how *Juliet* did get designed. Here is how Holland saw his part: "The essence of yacht design for us is to get into a client's head, interpret his vision. In this case he wanted sailing performance from us, and that was fairly well defined. So, we designed the basic shape, sailplan, rig, deck plan and proportions. Our office was less inhibited, because the client couldn't dictate the naval architecture of the underbody. Yes, he wanted to *know* about it, but not *define* it. From the start we were open to the idea of collaboration with someone who could provide the *texture* he wanted. I think Pieter had a harder time, as the client has a definite feeling for texture."

Beeldsnijder expresses parallel feelings: "Yacht design is an emotional act; if I get one million details right, but one is wrong, I am unhappy. It is a matter of creating what the owner has in mind to give a good feeling all around. I can take a design in a certain direction, but the lead must come from the client. In this case it was a strong lead. We were trying to find our way, and he never gave up the search for the best way. As the boat grew, his ideas grew, he wanted more all the time. If we went to dinner, we needed paper, napkins, tablecloths, anything to draw on. That was important because I design from the inside to the outside; there is a close relation between them that can't stop somewhere – not at crew quarters, lazarette, deck fittings, stairs, rig or hand rails. Design has many levels, many kinds of music; all must harmonize."

So the client was like a magnet, drawing the project together. Yet, Beeldsnijder and Holland, who have quite different magnetism of their own, have many more strong similarities. For one, as artists they are supremely self-critical. Holland admits that he could have given his *Whirlwind XII* a bit more sheer curve;

▲ *Pieter Beeldsnijder Design, Edam.*

Beeldsnijder went back and altered his schooner *Gloria*, because he was displeased with her bowsprit. And both men arrived at similar abstract notions of design that subconsciously strengthen the magnetism. "Every shape has its own aspect ratio," says Holland, "the relation between length, width and height; it attacks the eye differently." Beeldsnijder says, "I look at each design as an ellipse that defines its shape. Everything must fit within the ellipse, with defining points along the ellipse; if anything sticks out, it is visually out of balance." Pleasing aspect ratio? Balanced elliptics? Is this design-textbook hyperbole? Certainly not. For these attitudes, which neither man had ever shared with the other, were the base of the harmony that led to *Juliet*'s success.

But no one would be naive enough to say, in a project of such immensity, that the harmony was always consonant. There were disagreements, surely. At first the client was not entirely pleased with Holland's stern shape, which was quickly made right. And the frustrating see-saw effort that engaged Beeldsnijder in designing the superstructure and its crowning pilothouse would test any man's patience. Even the shipyard's many unique talents may have injected dissonance. Ron Holland finds Wolter Huisman's influence and strength unquestioned; he praises Wolter's ability to "sleep, eat and breathe every project." But he also was concerned that by developing, as it turned out, so many new systems – reel winches, steering, exhausts and more – the yard was adding project cost, not an unreasonable concern for a designer wishing his client to have one supremely affirmative experience and, possibly, more later.

But in the end it was the client, who willingly paid for the development, who said: "It was a good collaboration; they could each learn something from the other. The dialogue itself was the essence. We often found ourselves sitting around a dinner table, designing the boat as it was under construction. But the best element in the team is the yard. If Wolter Huisman weren't an enlightened man, it wouldn't work. He's a long-distance thinker. He never says 'No' to a new and difficult idea; it's always, 'We'll study it.' As a result, I didn't have to push, because there was no resistance to push against. I just did the creative directing to bring out the best in everyone; juices flowed, we took ideas from each other and we had a ball."

One recalls the trailblazing musician Arnold Schoenberg, inventor of the Twelve-Tone system of composing, creator of some of the century's most forward-looking works and a brilliant painter as well, who wrote that the artist "must open the valves in order to relieve the interior pressure of a creation ready to be born." With the creation of *Juliet*, the valves operated under a great deal of pressure but, as you will see, it brought forth a steady flow of ideas and a sailing yacht of rare and powerful distinction.

▲ *Ron Holland Design, Currabinny.*

HULL FORM

"And I must borrow every changing shape to find expression." – T.S. Eliot

In early 1988, when the client arrived in Europe, he had intended for *Juliet* to be modelled after Ron Holland's 103-foot *Whirlwind XII*. But over the next twelve months, after signing the letter of intent, he became totally immersed in the possibilities of machinery, space and comforts, and he encouraged her to blossom to 120, 130, 132, 135, then 142 feet and finally to 142 feet, 11 inches, into a slightly bigger sister to Holland's *Cyclos III*. "This was unique in my experience," Holland recalls, sitting in his airy, woody office – the attic of a converted stone farmhouse in Currabinny, County Cork, Ireland. "I never had a client who wanted a ninety-footer at the outset, who ended up with one hundred forty-three feet. Yes, they do tend to grow, but not *double*." [In terms of displacement, materials and cost, a 143-foot yacht is actually more than double a 90-footer.] Holland's design project manager Rob Jacob, however, who worked with him on *Juliet* and *Cyclos*, recalls that *Cyclos* played an even more significant role in their efforts: "Designing *Juliet* was relatively easy for us. We did all the tough work with *Cyclos*; she was our mockup."

Cyclos had indeed been a tough challenge for Holland and his staff, including his long-time number-crunching partner Butch Dalrymple-Smith. She was their largest project yet, and because she was designed for a client who demanded high performance above all else, Holland says, he had been required to draw a trim, efficient hull, with low freeboards, no bulwarks and a small low deckhouse; and he was "pushed for the best possible sailing shape." He found that shape, first, by developing a unique bulbed keel in the wind tunnel of the Royal Technical Institute of Stockholm, then testing it in conjunction with rudder designs and hull models at the University of Southampton towing tank. In this effort he worked closely with Prof. Jelle Gerritsma, a Delft University hydrodynamicist and technical advisor on the Huisman board of directors, who checked Holland's calculations for the hull balance and confirmed the expected helm loads. All observers, including her owner, agree that *Cyclos III* exceeded the sailing performance expected of her.

Juliet, whose hull lines evolved out of *Cyclos*'s superb shape, is nearly a meter longer overall, has a waterline of 115.51 feet (35.21 meters), a draft of 15 feet (4.58 meters) and a beam of 29.53 feet (9 meters), about 40 cm more than *Cyclos*. *Juliet* also has about eight percent more displacement and is surely more cruising oriented. So Holland augmented her shape and took the

▲ *Rob Jacob draws the lines* ▼ *The keel and bulb developing.*

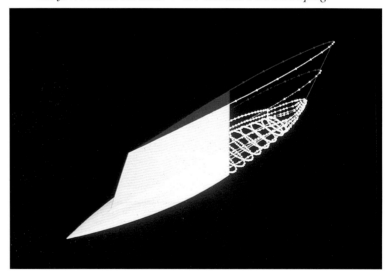

▼ *Number-cruncher Butch Dalrymple-Smith.*

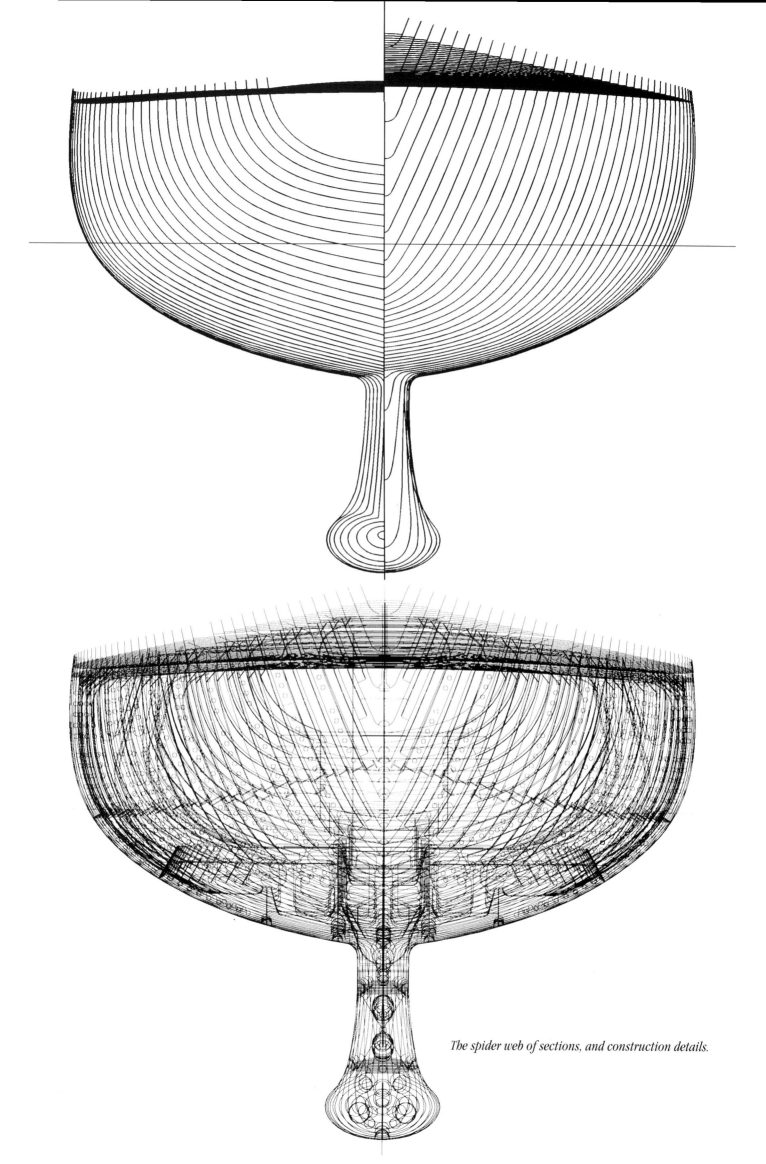

The spider web of sections, and construction details.

"edge" off her lines to suit her more stately purpose: He rounded her forefoot to reduce slamming; filled out the underbody aft for greater reaching power and interior volume and increased dead-rise aft to dampen those annoying slaps under the counter when she lays at anchor. As a result, Holland says, "where *Cyclos* is more clinical, *Juliet* is more rounded, traditional, substantial." Holland then prescribed a keel similar to the one he gave *Cyclos*, a relatively shoal fin with a high-efficiency elliptical bulb. But to accommodate the client's desire, he reduced the draft and added a bit more compensating ballast. He also added a touch more leading edge balancing flap to the rudder to assure a light, sensitive helm.

Another big difference between the two boats is that *Cyclos* has no furling systems; though she has superior windward performance, she also demands a certain degree of muscularity to set her sails. *Juliet* on the other hand has a full furling rig and totally machine-assisted sail handling. This obviously implies both added complexity and weight, yet Holland was able to take advantage of the Huisman experience in building *Cyclos* to alter *Juliet's* scantlings: Though larger, *Juliet* has only slightly more hull material, so she tolerates the additional ballast to counter the heavier superstructure, cruising gear and rig. "You can't have enough stability in a boat like this," says Holland.

Obviously, with all emphasis on comfort and stability, everyone's largest concern with *Juliet* was controlling her weight. It is almost a rule of thumb that a yacht grows beyond her design weight during construction: Gear is often added after the hull design is approved and components are upgraded in size; on the other hand, nothing ever seems to shrink or go away, and once the

boat is in the water unplanned payload items inevitably proliferate by the ton – *Juliet* carries three hard-bottom inflatables and a clinker-built sailing dinghy, just to cite one example. "That's a lesson that takes time to grasp after you have worked with racing boats," says Holland. "Most cruising boats don't have enough volume to carry the weight of equipment," so he made certain that *Juliet* does. Many shipyards, in fact, assume that designers are likely to underestimate displacement, so they allow an unofficial "fudge factor" for weight. At Huisman, the "fudge" is sweet and controlled: Weight calculations are constantly reviewed and a hull is weighed at critical stages in the construction. When it came time to pour *Juliet's* lead ballast the yard knew just how much she would need to meet her design stability and in which keel recesses it would go for proper trim.

Once *Juliet's* underbody took form, there remained the question of her hull profile above the waterline: her bow angle, stern shape and sheer, which combine to give a yacht her character and style. In discussing these design elements thoughtfully, Ron Holland frankly admits one of the lesser-known truths of his seemingly systematic profession: Naval architects shape a yacht by eye and by instinct, not by science. When pushed to be explicit, though, Holland recalls that in his early days, when he designed such renowned racers as the One-Tonner *Golden Apple*, *Imp*, Edward Heath's *Morning Cloud* and Jim Kilroy's maxi *Kialoa IV*, his bows usually made an arbitrary angle to the water in the 45-degree range. As he did more cruising yachts in the style of *Garuda*, *Sensation* and *Gleam*, the angle tended to become more acute, more refined, shifting the hull's shape away from a strict racing-

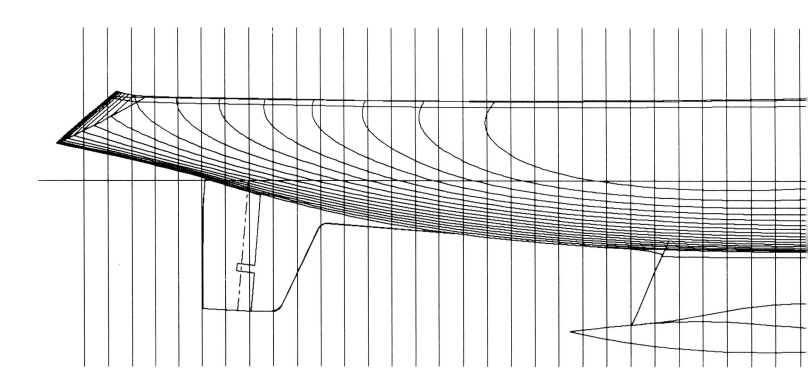

rule influence toward a personal and aesthetic one. *Juliet*'s bow makes a more graceful, perhaps more classic 38-degree angle with the water. That seven degrees not only adds almost a meter to her bow overhang, it gives her a profile that could never be confused with the blunt, homely products of the International Offshore Rule.

As to the sheer line, that mysterious three-dimensional curve along the rail that defines a hull's aura and excitement, the dilemma is greater. Here are two expert opinions on the matter of sheer: The designer/historian Howard Chapelle wrote: "The sheer of a yacht has much to do with her beauty, which in sailing craft … is based largely upon tradition." And Norman Skene, design theorist, wrote: "One can work one's heart out and make a design look well on paper, only to discover to one's horror that when the boat is first launched, she is an ugly duckling. Perhaps the one single line that crowns or damns the whole creation is the sheer line." Alas, neither of these great American authorities goes on to say precisely how a sheer becomes a *crown*, not a *damnation*. But Ron Holland reckons his own art as best he can this way: "Design is a two-dimensional representation of a three-dimensional object. It requires an uncanny ability to see in the mind's eye what the object will look like, then render it on a flat sheet of paper. Sometimes the results are awkward. There is something elusive about the sheer line, whose compound curvature can never be fully represented on a flat sheet. It's hard for a designer to say when it's right, but if it's wrong everyone knows it. You learn that you need more shape on paper than you think is right."

In the 1960s, Holland feels, cruisers evolved from IOR designs by architects who knew little else, who spent little time worrying about sheer and proportion. He, too, was more interested in such matters as weight, performance and engineering than aesthetics, and used standard rule-driven sheer lines. He attributes his current aesthetic awareness to his early experiments with models, which help a designer to visualize. But now most designers do their work with computers – Holland was a pioneer user of the Intergraph system. Now he says. "We can isolate and overlay design elements; we can see how they change when the boat heels, how certain lines get distorted, others stay sweet. There is less excuse to get it wrong. But even with a computer it's still very difficult to read a sheer line: The curved screen distorts it and you are back to aesthetic square one. It's always a value judgment; you have to check it on paper."

When they were pleased by *Juliet*'s design parameters, Holland and Rob Jacob did indeed check that the lines were "fair," that the delicate web of sections, waterlines, diagonals and buttocks – the arcane curves that define a hull's shape – would produce a smooth curvature, with no discontinuities. Ironically, Holland, who is sometimes too modest, sees much of his work as just a repeat of history: "Go to the New York Yacht Club model room and you will see all aspects of design have been done before; there's no new angle, no new curve, no new idea. Nathanael Herreshoff probably did it first." Herreshoff may or may not have done it first, but even without a computer he surely did it faster – his yachts number in the thousands. But, when Ron Holland delivered his final set of hull, keel and rudder lines to the Huisman shipyard, that was only the beginning of *Juliet*'s long, animated and extravagant design process.

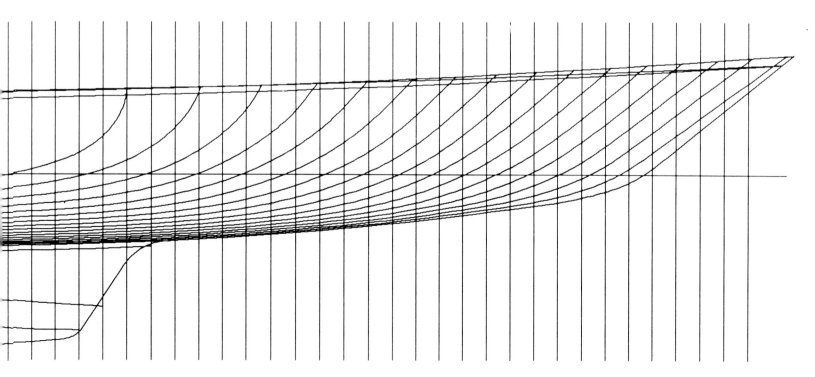

▲ *The graceful hull profile and elusive sheer.*

Juliet: Specifications

Naval Architecture:	Ron Holland Design	Displacement:	254 tonnes / 560.000 pounds
Styling / Interior Design:	Pieter Beeldsnijder Design	Ballast:	65 tonnes / 144.000 pounds
Builder:	Royal Huisman Shipyard	Ballast/Displacement:	26%
		Sail Area (working):	887 meters^2 / 9.543 feet^2
Length Overall:	43.58 meters / 142.99 feet	Sail Area (light):	700 meters^2 / 7.530feet^2
Length On Waterline:	35.21 meters / 115.51 feet	Sail Area (total):	1.587 meters^2 / 17.073 feet^2
Beam, Maximum:	9 meters / 29.53 feet	Main Mast Height Above Water:	48.66 meters / 159.6 feet
Draft:	4.58 meters / 15 feet	Mizzen Mast Height Above Water:	33.44 meters / 109.7 feet

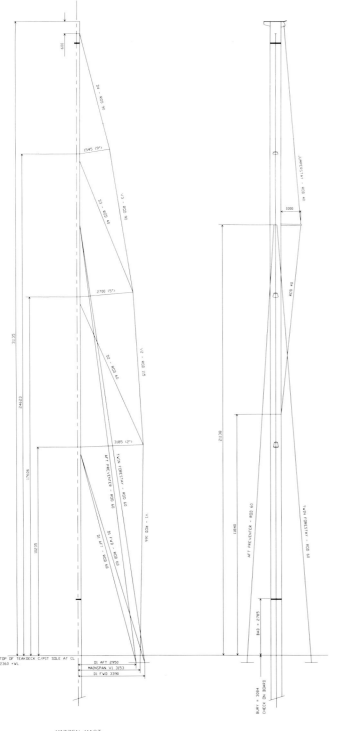

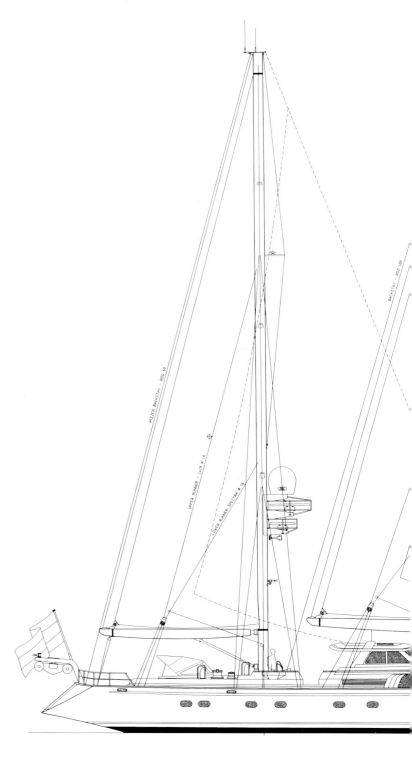

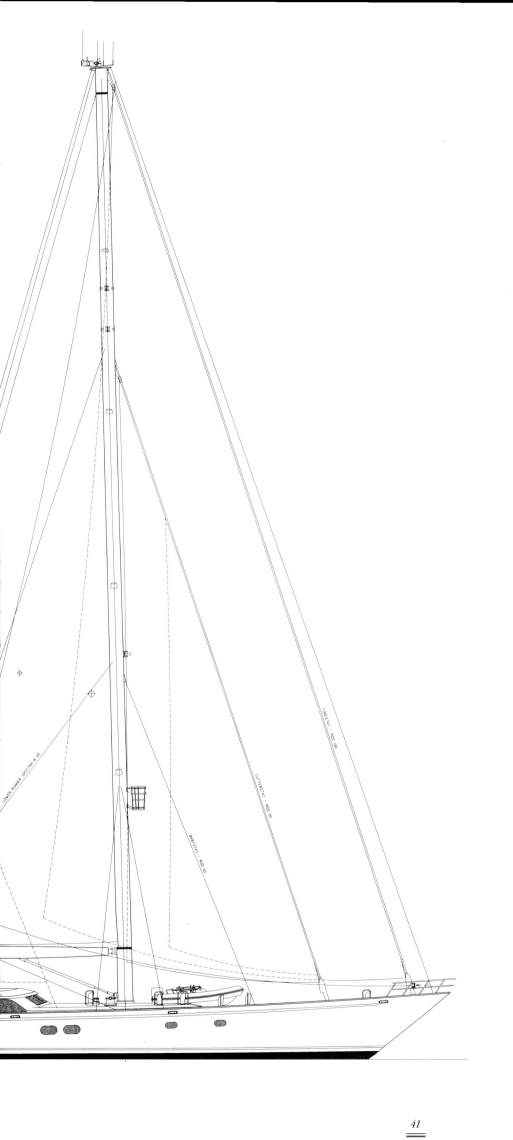

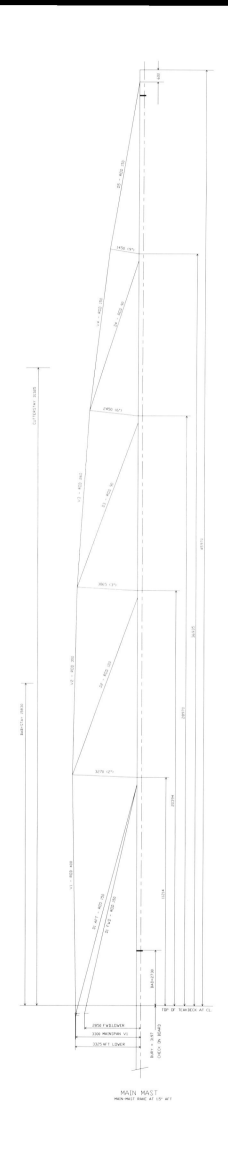

MAIN MAST
MAIN-MAST RAKE AT 1.5° AFT

41

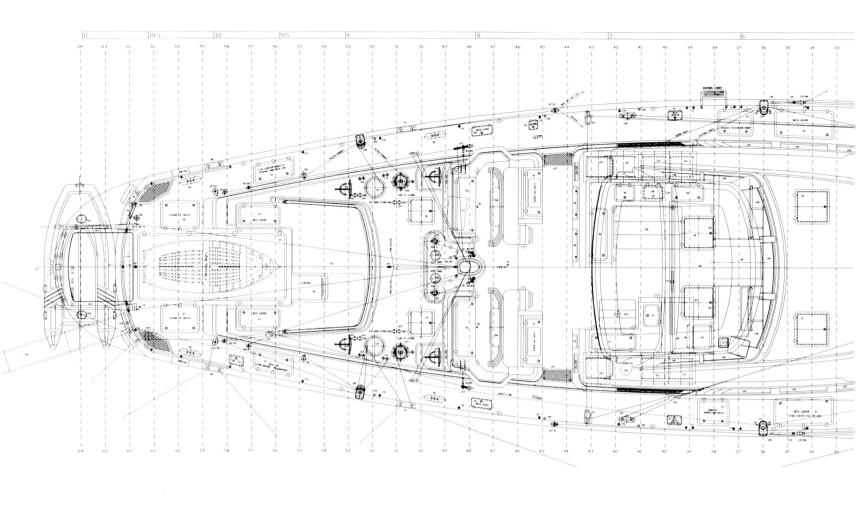

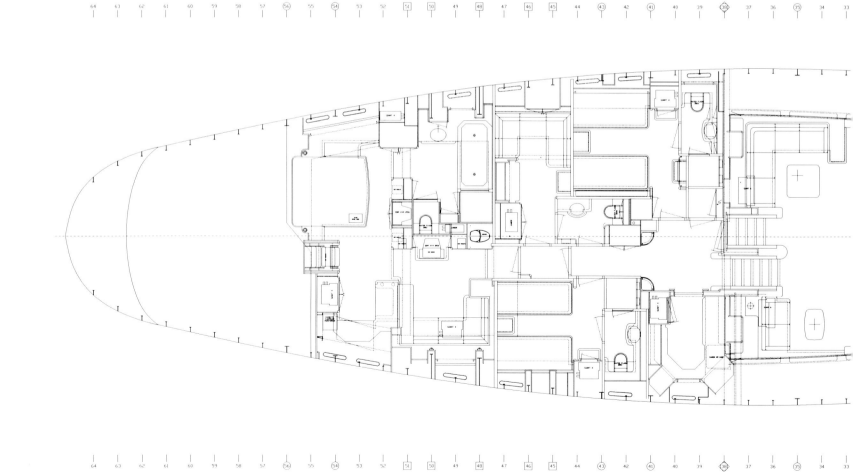

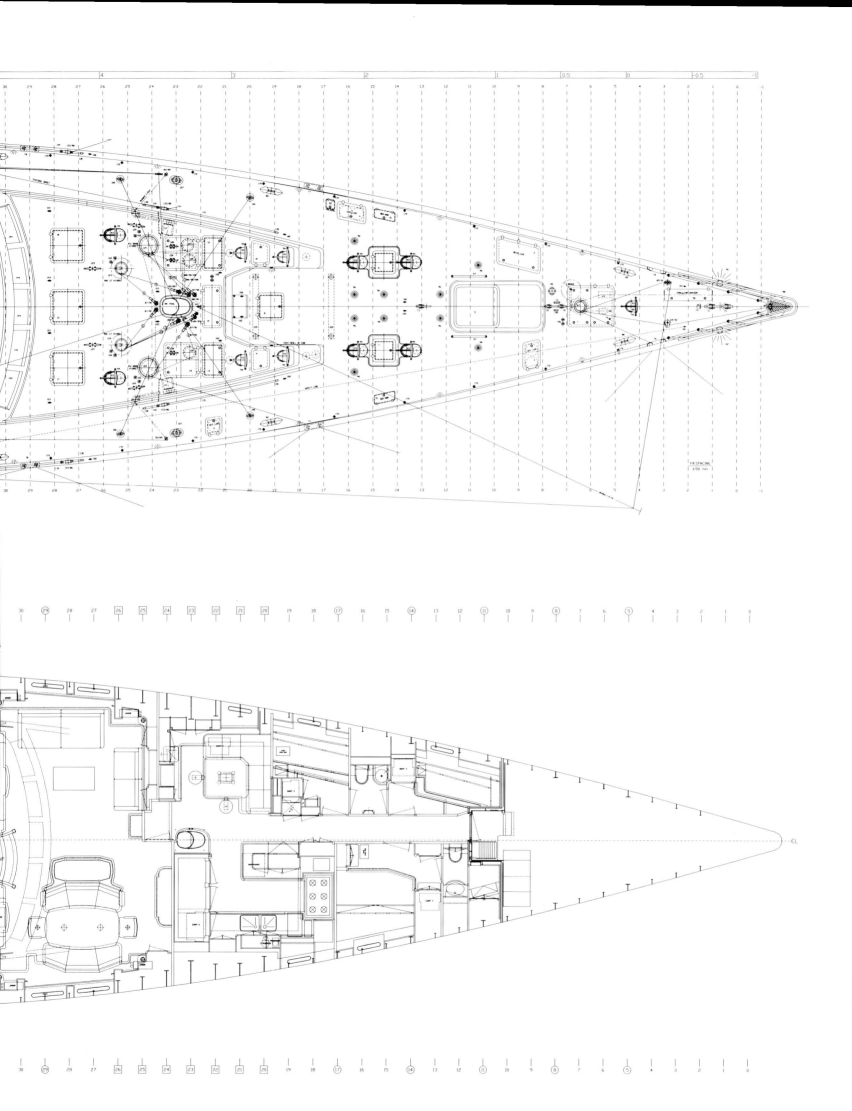

ABOVE THE WATERLINE

*"The physician can bury his mistakes, but the architect can only
advise his client to plant vines." – Frank Lloyd Wright*

How should a sailboat look? Clipper-bowed and American
as *Ticonderoga*? Plum-bowed and fantailed as a Bristol Channel
pilot cutter? Flush-decked and razor-fine as a 10-Meter? Balanced
and substantial as John Alden's *Malabar X*? Boot-like as a junk or
certain Taiwan-built motorsailers? The choice is infinite each time a
new project is initiated. Hear our client trying to make his choice:
"I was tempted at first to do her in a classic style, but I was afraid
enough modernity would creep in to ruin the look." He did give
Ron Holland and Pieter Beeldsnijder a general, somewhat
conservative, compass heading somewhere between classic and
modern when he expressed admiration for Philip Rhodes's
"timeless look," though he wanted "less straight-sidedness, more
fluidity in the house." He specified a trim profile, but also insisted
on a pilothouse, which can mitigate trimness. This knotty balancing
act challenged Holland somewhat at the outset.

But, it was Beeldsnijder who bore the heavier weight of
the responsibility: with the concurrent interior design also in his
lap, it plunged him into four years' worth of high-speed, all-season
220-km round-trip commutes from his Edam studio to meetings at
the Huisman yard, a routine he was fortunately accustomed to from
having already collaborated there on *Huaso*, *Ebb Tide*, *Cyclos II*,
Hetairos, *Volador*, *Happy Joss* and *Metolius*.

In more than 30 years as a naval architect and designer,
Beeldsnijder, whose prematurely gray head belies a youthful approach to life, has several hundred complete motorboat and sailing
yacht designs to his credit. He studied naval architecture and interior design, worked with Robert Clark and the de Vries Lentsch
office, and did every sort of marine-related work from lofting,
machining and metalworking to fabricating yacht furniture. His
most recognizable triumphs are the schooner *Gloria*, Hakvoort's
first motoryacht, *Tonga*, the 50-meter *Jefferson Beach* and yachts
for the royal families of Holland, Spain and Greece. But he's also
designed fishing trawlers and a super
North Sea seine purser.

To achieve the style that the
client sought in *Juliet*, Beeldsnijder first
studied Holland's hull and superstructure design to grasp their dynamic.
Though Holland had prescribed bulwarks for *Juliet*, for various reasons

Beeldsnijder felt the hull needed a touch more sheer curve. He
doesn't like even a suggestion of a flush deck "from which you fall
into a hole to go below," or a superstructure standing "nakedly" on
it. So he raised the bulwarks to "sink the superstructure so that it
appears to grow out of the deck." As a bonus, raising the bulwarks
honed the bow overhang, which balances the transom ideally, even
as *Juliet* heels and gains sailing length.

Rob Jacob of the Holland office appreciated the changes:
"*Cyclos* has a trim, beautiful look, but no bulwarks. *Juliet*'s
bulwarks put an edge on the boat, give a safe feeling, allow you to
walk around her deck. Even while under construction, when her
deck was so high off the ground, the difference was dramatic."

A superstructure, like the sheer, is also basic to a yacht's
character. As drawn by Ron Holland it was a modern big-boat
configuration: a low forward section over the crew quarters, galley
and saloon, and an upper level enclosing the deckhouse, with a
pilothouse dodger atop that. It was up to Beeldsnijder to refine its
shape and introduce detail that harmonized with the sheer and his
developing interior design. As a result, his superstructure is enriched by the interplay of bevels, curves and long straight lines.
There are subtle relations among the bow and transom angles,
window shapes, mainsheet arch, coamings and ventilator slots: As
the eye moves from the bow or stern toward the center, bevels become increasingly more vertical, in pyramid-like steps, until the
bold angle of the mainsheet arch towers above it all.

Beeldsnijder struggled long with that arch's aesthetic,
drawing it vertically at first, then canting it aft, and finally forward
to get the right profile. Does Beeldsnijder calculate and draw these
angles consciously to satisfy some rule? No: "It just has to be pleasing," he says. Of course, the more "pleasing" it became, by virtue
of its interwoven curves and bisecting forms, the tougher the
superstructure was for the Huisman yard to engineer and build.

The cockpit structure was no
easier; it was designed a dozen times. As
the client said: "We tried to reinvent the
cockpit. A cockpit must be fun. You
can't just put two benches and a table
on centerline and call it a cockpit. It has

◄ *The bulwark-enhanced sheer.*

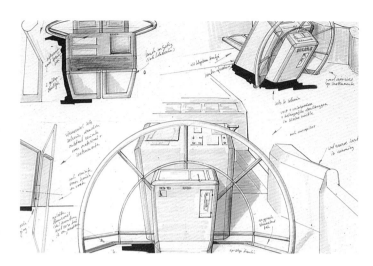

to be a small outdoor living room. We wanted an open passageway across it, but also a way of keeping children inside and safe. We considered the seats: their height, roundness of front corners and back angles; we even thought of strong gimballed couches that stay level when the boat heels. We wanted a place for sunglasses, which get sat upon with no dignity. We wanted lockers for shoes – if thirty people come aboard where do we stow sixty shoes plus boots?"

The cockpit finally became three spaces, each with a purpose: The forward one, under the pilothouse roof, is first intended for standing watch, but also for casual entertaining. Abaft the owner's companionway, under the mizzen boom, a teak-decked lounge surrounded by cushion-covered seats is for private sunning or sleeping under the stars. Between them stands the steering cockpit, on a raised deck split by the mizzen mast. This crucial space, which is a marvel of engineering as well as aesthetics, began from one overriding premise: twin outboard wheels (a large single wheel placed on centerline would have cut deeply into the deck and encroached on the living space below). But it was also essential for the helmsman to have easy communication with the sail trimmers, observe the "slot" between headsails and main, and see forward without being forced to crane, perch on coamings or stand on a seat. The solution came to the client in a flash of inspiration: Extend the helm seats outboard, beyond the coaming perimeters, onto small balconies that hang over the side decks.

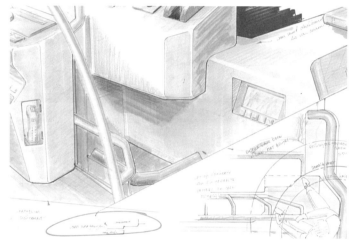

It is a refreshing solution that works: Seated in the balconies the helmsman can see around the deckhouse or through the pilothouse windows to view the bow, other vessels and the oncoming sea. As a result of this design, the pedestals also turned into unique constructs. They are split in two sections: the forward, larger parts have a radar repeater and chart navigator (with motorized covers), engine instrumentation and gyrocompass, with separate sets of engine throttle and thruster joysticks on a convenient outboard panel in front of the balcony seat. The smaller aft sections each hold a Robertson autopilot, with "takeover" button for steering from either station. Each 1.95-meter wheel spins in the gap between the sections, with spokes that bend aft over the autopilot to align their rim perfectly with the seat.

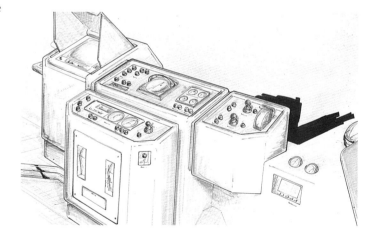

All this cramming of the client's eccentric, ergonomic, social and technical desires into one sailboat cockpit was a monstrous undertaking, necessitating weeks of design culminated by the erecting of a complete plywood mockup for study of all the components. A mockup is a full-size construct that allows full-size people to bump into their full-size mistakes before they are welded into a full-size hull; it was the only way to assure the client that his outdoor life would match is inner needs.

But no mockup had yet been produced that would give credence to the icing on the superstructure cake: the pilothouse

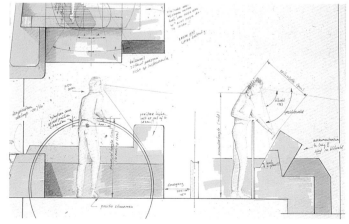

▲ *Before reality: ergonomics and design studies.*

▲ *The steering-cockpit mockup: harmony in plywood.*

▲ *The profile: collaboration in sculpted metal.*

structure. The pilothouse on a modern sailing yacht is no longer just a corner for the watch to tuck into out of the weather. It is a social corner as well. With all that must be crammed into its shell, its shape can make or break a yacht's profile. The client sought a well-designed, solid structure that would have, as he said, "an open look like a sports car, but afford absolute protection like a tank." The permutations and combinations were, as usual, almost without number: A folding dodger, a windscreen only and a glass bubble were studied; various styles of window openings, ventilation and windshield wipers were weighed; cold-molded wood and stainless steel were considered for construction. And each solution had to carefully consider the mainsheet arch, which is placed strategically and monumentally in the middle of the action. It was also a tension-filled search because the client sensed undercurrents of resistance at the yard toward the very *idea* of a pilothouse. (Early on, Beeldsnijder had drawn an outrageous shape the client called "the ugliest thing I've ever seen," until he realized it had been playfully done to dissuade him. It didn't.)

In May 1992, with the hull being faired, joinery well along and fewer than eight months to the scheduled commissioning, a highly energized late-night meeting was held. With a spirit of excitement in the air, Beeldsnijder tried a number of ideas and finally achieved the elusive shape that now crowns *Juliet*'s profile: a handsome hardtop with a gently cambered roof, angled windows and a long overhang; a true pilothouse, a fine lounge, a work of art. But it was only a shape on paper. Someone had to design its structure, draw its parts and make it work with the mainsheet arch: Jurrie Zandbergen. Zandbergen is the Huisman construction, deck and rigging project manager on whose shoulders and drawing board fall the detailing of such odd but essential features. By this time, of course, the mainsheet arch was already in place, an integral part of the boat. In designing the arch earlier, had Zandbergen's engineering prevailed over the client's aesthetics, it would have been heavier, and the mechanical design of the pilothouse therefore easier. Now, if the pilothouse were to be welded to the arch, the mainsheet load might flex the arch slightly, which would normally be acceptable, but in this case it would unduly stress the pilothouse. Zandbergen considered leaving a gap between them, to prevent the motion from being transferred, but careful analysis proved the arch rigid enough, and he designed the house to be welded to the arch.

Still, it took six months to finish the drawings, loft and cut the parts and build the pilothouse, a function of the shortfall in databases for such one-of-a-kind designs. When it was finally welded in place, Zandbergen, admiring the results, reflected on the client's *persona*: "He invites you to do crazy things." The crazy, but solid, pilothouse was finished just in time for *Juliet*'s transfer, in November 1992, to the paint shed for her final cosmetic work.

▲ *The proof of the mockup is in the steering.*

SAILING ... ON DRY LAND

"The debt we owe to the play of imagination is incalculable." – C.C. Jung

In the year 1174, Bonanno Pisano began to build an ornate marble tower in his native town of Pisa when he noted, too late to do anything about it, that there was soil instability under its foundation; Italy is still trying to keep his leaning Pisan gem from collapsing into the dust. In 1940, the four-month old Tacoma Narrows Bridge did indeed collapse, because engineers had overlooked the potentially serious effects of local winds on the span's natural resonance. The new 1984 Pontiac Fiero had so many design flaws it prompted one witty critic to inquire if General Motors had ever bothered to test one of the autos *outdoors*. These designer headaches could well have been averted by better, clearer planning.

Planning of systems, machinery and operating procedures on a new yacht is equally essential, particularly as it affects safe, efficient operation – nothing can be left to chance once the yacht is launched. Planning these elements on very large, very complicated yachts presents special challenges today, as they are carrying more and more machinery that must be run by fewer and fewer crew. That machinery, therefore, must be low-maintenance and user-friendly; those systems must rely on computers for many routine operations and those procedures must be easily grasped by the crew to avoid dangerously emotional decision-making under stressful circumstances. To accomplish all this well in advance, Huisman project managers and a yacht's key crew members go through a process of error-avoidance commonly called "dry sailing." Dry sailing is a form of therapy in which the group operates the yacht in its collective imagination, to anticipate all possibilities and design for them. Without this foresight a crew can later be dangerously overworked; yet even with it, the equal danger of crew complacency must be considered. (Ron Holland has warned that proper crew training was the naval architect's last hurdle in assuring successful large-yacht designs.)

Huisman dry sailing comprises freewheeling brain-storming sessions that often run long after the yard cleaning staff has gone home, and frequently spill over into the little "Mekong" restaurant across the road, where the Vietnamese specialties and good Dutch beer enhance the thought process. Dry sailing is basically sitting around a table and asking, repeatedly, "What if?"

▲ *A Huisman designer double-checks lines.*

What if you have to jibe all-standing unexpectedly? *What if* there's a galley fire? *What if* the steering fails? *What if* the main engine raw-water pump packs in?

What if, for example, *Juliet's* crew wants to tack under full sail? Jurrie Zandbergen's answer is: "You can't tack this boat in one movement: shout *Hard alee!*, turn the wheel and go." First, there is too much sail area and running rigging for a small crew to contend with. But even with enough crew, the hydraulics haven't the power to ease and trim genoa, staysail, main and mizzen all at once. The crew must tack in orderly stages: furl some sail, tack, trim and unfurl as is common to big boats. To help set the pattern, Zandbergen and two other world-class dry sailors, Jan Bokxem (systems and electronics project manager) and Sam Bos (chief systems engineer), took *Juliet* "out to sea" on imaginary calm days and windy nights. Then they said: *Let's tack to see if anyone says: "Hey! You can't use that winch because you'll take power from my winch!"* Noting all the resulting combinations, they distributed the most frequently used functions to the eight prime hydraulic pumps and spread the others to avoid conflict. Now, the power consumption is limited and there are no "dead knobs" (functions sacrificing power to other functions).

They also divided the sail-trim functions so that port and starboard consoles control winches only on their respective sides. There is no cross-linking that would encourage one crew member to try to do everything, so two crew are generally needed during a tack or jibe to keep their eyes on the results (an unobserved ten-ton sheet winch can do major damage in seconds). To further enhance safety, the dry sailors assigned joysticks for trimming and knobs for furling, separated by ridges and corresponding to the bow-to-stern order of the sails; a crew can manipulate the correct control, even in dark of night, and concentrate on the result. As Zandbergen says: "No one of us knows everything, but together we know a lot. I like dry sailing. You close your eyes to *see* the boat sailing and ask, *What am I doing? What are the other guys doing?* and you design accordingly."

These standard brainstorming sessions were each organized to solve particular problems. But in a broad sense, *every* general planning meeting held among the Huisman staff, beginning in the spring of 1988, was a form of dry sailing in which many details were argued and decided. Nothing on *Juliet* – not a hatch, jockey pole, radar screen or coffee maker – appears by default; each was selected in a meeting with the client, the designers, Jens Cornelsen, Wolter, commercial director Evert van Dishoeck, a mix of project managers and two other important attendees: Herb Kiendl and Paddy Lynch. Kiendl is *Juliet's* captain; Lynch is, for want of a more deserving title, chief yacht administrator. They are both professional crew of the highest caliber. They had run *Ebb Tide* for the client until he sold her, then hung up their boots to participate in *Juliet's* planning from a crew office in the yard. The difference between them and the project managers is that these two

▲ *Jan Bokxem and Jurrie Zandbergen plan winch controls.*

world-class sailors are now at sea enjoying the fruits of the long dry-sailing meetings they contributed to.

Careful minutes were taken at those meetings, as they became guidance for most of the detail that makes *Juliet* unique. A quick survey of those minutes, numbering in the hundreds of pages, and weighing several kilos, may give the reader some insight into the give and take that led to *Juliet*'s many pieces coming relentlessly, but perfectly together:

14 Oct. 1988:

Five months after the letter of intent was signed, a **120-foot** sloop was considered: building to begin December 1988. Requirements: A battery boat; garage space for an Avon inflatable, bicycles, windsurfers, two 50-cc motorbikes, water skis, spare dinghy. Prof. Gerritsma to do calculations for construction, weight, speed prediction, keel.

2 Feb. 1989:

Holland and Beeldsnijder agree to collaborate on a **132-foot** ketch, draft 14 feet for shallow Pacific harbors, Beam$_{max}$ 28.54 feet (8.7 m); a model commissioned for study. Client asks for full-width galley/crew mess, bathtub, transom garage. Seaway, Barient and Lewmar captive winches are studied; opening hull ports eliminated.

17 Feb. 1989:

A **130-foot** ketch displacing 215/220 tons was reviewed and considered "definite." Beeldsnijder provides hull profile and deck plan; Holland a lines plan. A "cooperative" winch arrangement shown. New interior styling defined: "Lots of teak applied on white panels."

14 Apr. 1989:

"This meeting was organized to work out a **135-foot** center-cockpit ketch." Seats needed "to make steering a pleasant experience." Hydraulic cockpit seating, Hundested propeller tabled. Study sketches shown for: galley, wood panel style, dinghy stowage, deck hatch, boarding platform, caprail, rubrail and sheer (some in whimsical hand). Preliminary sketch of new hull: LOA **142.76 feet**.

18 May 1989:

The **135-footer** discussed; also new dimensions: LOA **142.7 feet**; Beam 29.2 feet; Draft 14.99 feet. Steering with twin wheels, rudder motor discussed. Client asks to mount a large ship model in saloon, store 400 music CDs, have master light switches for every cabin, a lower superstructure than *Cyclos*, an elevating mainmast crow's nest.

11 July 1989:

General arrangement reviewed. Dodgers over companionways noted as "critical to the look." Hull ports, bathroom floor heating, radar and sonar, deckhouse furniture reviewed; comparison made between British and US nautical charts to dimension the chart table. Sketches submitted: swim platform, tender stowage and saloon.

▲ *Wolter and his design team study the sail-control panel.*

13/14 Sept. 1989:

Second model shown; note made: "The feeling of the yacht is to be *new classic*, sculpted alloy, trimmed with natural and varnished teak and white painted vertical surfaces." Approval of keel, rudder and skeg given. Prof. Gerritsma gives analysis of **142.76-foot** ketch, with Delft University velocity predictions (cost: 4,000 Dutch guilders). Preliminary weights: hull and superstructure 46,000 kilos; ballast 60,000 kilos; batteries 7,000 kilos; masts 6,000 kilos.

28 Sept. 1989:

A new model presented. Client approves hull lines, deck plans, general arrangement, styling, engine, generator sets, systems, electronics and electrics. More sketches discussed. Numeriek Centrum [computer house] consulted for the first time. Cost calculation begun based on proposed systems and ketch rig: LOA **142.99 feet** (43.58 m).

By November 1989, with *Juliet*'s length at last fixed, there was no backing away: Drawings were begun in several locales and a flood of information poured in from suppliers and consultants. In the next series of meetings, interior impressions, engineering drawings of the lazarette, studies of davits, cleats, bollards, turning blocks and deck gear appear in the minutes. In spring 1990, just as welders began to piece *Juliet* together, the "classic" interior was evolving, with a teak foreship and mahogany aft. Electronic schematics were drawn and a deck lobster box was proposed. In

September 1990 details of a grand saloon staircase, owner's suite and entertainment systems were submitted. The navigation room and its incredible contents took shape. By the end of 1990 crew quarters were approved and a toaster was selected. By January 1991, *opening* portlights, alarms and Rondal's reel winches and runner system were approved, as were seating, helm balconies, transom stairs, gangway and coaming shapes.

In these meeting notes one can also find a cornucopia of proposals, many brilliant and original, that were scrapped, and out of which one could build an entirely different yacht: It would be a 120-foot sloop with an all-teak interior, a transom garage, a full-width galley, off-the-shelf reel winches, canvas dodgers, sealed hull ports and 9,000 amp-hours of batteries. But, through it all – through the tensions and worries about the project's growing complexity, through the jockeying between client and shipyard as they came – cautiously at first, then ardently – to know each other's needs and capacities, no one lost a sense of humor. The meeting minutes are filled with sketches, doodles and cartoons to prove it, all spontaneous, all nonsense, all clues to the profound human element so essential to the volcanic, interactive human process of bringing forth a great machine, a great yacht.

• ● •

But *Juliet* soon had to be drawn in earnest, with absolute precision, the key to her being built. Who, exactly, drew her? You might as well ask: Who built the pyramids, who wrote the Bible, or

▲ *Wolter and Herb Kiendl discuss the primary winch cabinets.*

who painted Horta's fabled seawall? The answer in each case: Lots of folks. Ron Holland and Rob Jacob drew her on a computer screen; Pieter Beeldsnijder rendered her by hand, reserving his 630-megabyte computer for structural detail; machinery suppliers sent the yard precisely dimensioned drawings for space planning; each of the Huisman project managers drew her systems schematics and details; draftsmen worked up the structure and furniture at computer stations. Indeed, with its database potential the computer is a wondrous tool for shaping a yacht: it allows a designer to alter a shape, see it from all angles and learn whether everything needed will fit into that shape. Using the yard's AutoCAD system, with its great database of hull design, draftsmen were able, therefore, to draw the hull and deck structures in only a few months. But a computer can't do everything; it needs that database. The superstructure, therefore, for which there is no database, took them a year of hand drawing.

Discounting notepad sketches, coffee-stained discussion doodles, preliminary drawings, napkin and tablecloth art laundered forever down the drain, the portfolio of *Juliet*'s drawings is enormous: 103 drawings were needed for the hull shape and construction; 123 for the superstructure; 26 for the steering system; 37 for diverse deck gear (from pulpits to diving board); 20 for the anchoring system and 400 drawings were needed just for interior joinery, many with several sub-drawings per sheet. But there were times in the process where a drawing, or even a series of them

would not suffice to demonstrate a complex design, and scale models were commissioned for the client's approval. A model is after all an advanced form of drawing, a three-dimensional illustration confirming how shapes, details, even colors work together. But sometimes even a model could not satiate the client's immense hunger for ergonomic perfection, so a full-scale mockup, the *ultimate* form of drawing, was commissioned and built. In addition to the mockup of the steering cockpit, the yard made some equally extensive (and no less expensive) plywood mockups of the galley and crew mess, the navigation and engine rooms. The client asserted throughout that these mockups were among his best investments, because each time one was built, then walked in or sat upon, it helped edge *Juliet* closer to his dream of perfection. His enthusiasm for the remarkable results of this mockup-making process was so great that he once asserted: "If we were willing to spend hundreds of thousands of dollars on design, how could we *not* be willing to spend fifty thousand on mockups?"

Centuries from now archaeologists may dig up those decaying plywood mockups, plus all the non-biodegradable Mylar drawings and long lasting high-gloss models, and perhaps those mysterious artifacts will give them insight into how 20th-Century man built his fine ships. At any rate, by the spring of 1990, the shipyard's many file cabinets overflowed with two-dimensional drawings, indisputable evidence that *Juliet* was ready to take three-dimensional form.

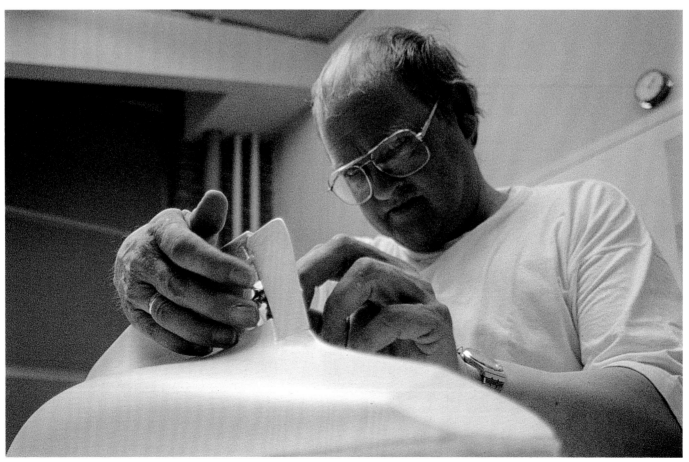

▲ *Roel Zwiers, Huisman's crafty modelmaker.*

THE JIGSAW PUZZLE

"Materials are indifferent. But the use we make of them is not a matter of indifference." – Epictetus

Aluminum: Atomic number 13; atomic weight 26.9815; melts at 660.2° C; boils at 2,467° C. Aluminum is the most abundant metal in the earth's crust yet, oddly, it is never found alone, only in combination with other elements: Its oxides (often called *alumina*) form the natural abrasive corundum, they are mined in the ore bauxite and, when infused with certain chance impurities, they are lustily sought as precious rubies and sapphires. Aluminum was discovered in 1825 by Hans Oersted, a Danish physicist; in the 1840s it was isolated as a powder, in the 1850s in chunks. Introduced at the 1855 Paris World's Fair it glittered like silver, but at $1,200 per kilo was more dear than gold. In 1866, Charles M. Hall, an American, extracted it by electrolytic reduction and by 1940 the price plummeted to thirty cents per kilo: aluminum became the material of choice for cookware, aircraft, chewing gum wrappers and, now, even baseball bats.

The first aluminum sailing yacht, a ten-meter canoe with a spritsail rig, was built in Europe around 1890. The first American boats – 18-footers one-fifth the weight of their wood equivalents – served the 1894 Wellman Polar Expedition. In 1931, the first "big" alloy yacht, the 55-foot express cruiser *Diana II*, was built in England and ever since shipyards have enjoyed aluminum's many advantages: It is half the weight of steel for equal structural strength; it is hard, uniform and ductile; it is easy to cut, drill, machine, grind, rivet, extrude and bend into complex shapes; it absorbs impact and resists corrosion; it is non-sparking, non-magnetic, non-absorbent and worm-proof. Among its few disadvantages are that it requires unique welding skills (not difficult to master) and it tends toward electrolytic activity with other metals (readily overcome by commonsense building practices).

Juliet's aluminum was manufactured on the western edge of Germany, in the 2,000-year-old city of Koblenz, where the Mosel joins the Rhine on its sinuous 1,320-kilometer drift from the Bodensee to Rotterdam. There, in a sprawling modern facility, Hoogovens Aluminium GmbH creates a wide variety of tailored aluminum products. The Hoogovens Koblenz facility was built in 1964 by the American giant Kaiser Aluminum, which sold it in 1987 to Hoogovens Groep, a multinational

Dutch steel maker, now Europe's fourth-largest aluminum producer. After expansions, the Koblenz facility now makes custom aluminum plate, sheet and extruded stock for construction, heat exchangers, transport tanks and the Airbus, and is the only German-based supplier of aluminum to the aerospace industry. The typical cycle of Hoogovens product begins at one of its smelting plants in Holland, Germany or Canada, where aluminum ore, brought from mines as far afield as Australia, is processed into near-pure ingots. Those ingots are shipped to Koblenz, re-melted in giant furnaces and combined by induction with select elements to create 100 special-purpose alloys that are re-cast into ingots for processing, accounting for 120,000 metric tons annually.

Juliet's structural and shell plate, for example, is 5083/H321, an alloy of magnesium and manganese formulated for tensile strength, good welding and resistance to seawater; her extruded stock is 6061-T6, an alloy of magnesium, copper and silicon for strength, hardness and extrudability. To make suitable plates, Hoogovens pre-heats ingots to 500° C and passes them back and forth between gargantuan steel rollers in a 3,800-ton hot-rolling mill. Each pass progressively lengthens and flattens the ingot, from about 600 mm down to as little as 3 mm, generating a thunderous rumbling as the rollers collide with the ingot, and sibilant hissing as liquid coolant boils away to a mist. When the mist clears, there remains gleaming finished plate, which is then "stretched" on an 8,000-ton rack to relieve internal stresses induced by such brute-force treatment. To create other forms, such as "T" sections, cylindrical billets of alloy are pre-heated to 570° C and squeezed in a giant press with up to 3,750 tons of force through a series of hardened dies, emerging as long, slender ribbons of precisely shaped extrusion.

But, through its Dutch distributor, BV Imco-Holland, Hoogovens supplies only stock. For the shaping of *Juliet*'s pieces the scene shifted in early 1990 from Koblenz to Numeriek Centrum Groningen (NCG), in Holland's industrial north. NCG is a sort of computer halfway-house between naval architects and shipyards all over the

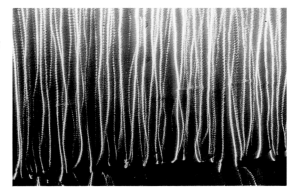

◄ *Gleaming, abundant aluminum.*

▲ *Hoogovens hot-rolls plate to the sound of thunder.*

world. Its task was to convert Ron Holland's hull lines and construction details, sent on a floppy disc, into computer drawings for cutting the thousands of parts from flat aluminum stock. To accomplish this, NCG first digitally translated Holland's data to their own computer system and rechecked the hull's fairing to be certain nothing was lost in the translation. Then they made computer models of each part, fairing it at full size to within 0.1 mm to assure its proper fit. They also drew up a table of offsets (reducing the design to numbers for the Huisman lofting team) and full-size Mylar mold-loft drawings for the yard to check parts against. And they designed and positioned the thousands of circular holes to be cut from frames, stringers and girders, which lighten them up to 20 percent without compromising their strength.

NCG also designed the mosaic of shell plates that form *Juliet*'s skin, a computer juggling act that must strike a balance between the desire for many small plates to idealize the shape, against the need for few large plates to minimize welding. Arriving at a shell comprising 160 plates, NCG then prepared careful bending instructions for Huisman workers to form each plate into *Juliet*'s continuum of compound curves, and made templates to check the curvatures. Then, in a computer operation that almost defies description, NCG prepared the "nesting" plans for cutting all the components out of their respective plate material. Like a model airplane kit or a paper doll's paper wardrobe, the nesting program squeezes the most parts onto each plate, minimizing costly scrap.

Juliet began to exist then, but only in megabyte models and Mylar maps. That was when Numeriek's sister division, Centraalstaal, took over. Centraalstaal, which processes 25,000 metric tons of steel and 300 of aluminum per year, is a major supplier of pre-cut ship "kits" for tankers, coasters, fishing trawlers and uncommon projects such as a 17th-century ship replica for Japan or the (abandoned) "Trump yacht." Centraalstaal cut out each of *Juliet*'s pieces by following NCG's digitized program, which guided its plasma cutter over each plate following the nesting pattern. The cutter head injected an 80,000-volt potential through the metal in a nitrogen-stabilized atmosphere, and the resulting plasma (an ethereal flow of subatomic particles neither solid, liquid nor gas) heated the metal along a thin line to almost 30,000° C, vaporizing it, letting each part drop free until only a skeleton plate remained. Plasma cutting may not be the most savory process in the industrial world – it takes place in a pool of unappetizing, murky cooling water – but with its stellar heat and celestial blue light it produces clean, hard-edged shapes, just what *Juliet* needed to begin taking form. The parts were numbered, strapped to pallets and shipped off to Vollenhove.

• • •

▲ *Centraalstaal plasma cutting.* ▼ *Willem Alves lofting.*

▼ *A final check before welding.*

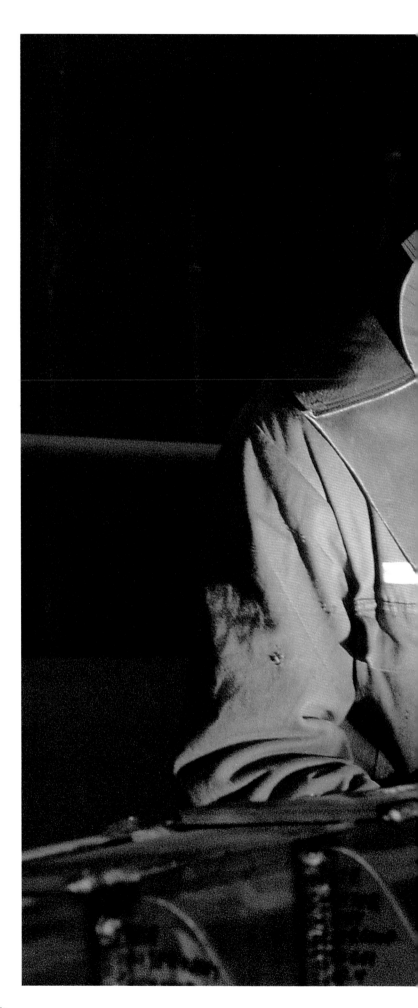

In May 1990, twenty-six months (and about as many meetings) after the client first walked into Wolter Huisman's office, welders finally fired up their gear to begin joining the pieces. But a modern aluminum hull is not built like an old wooden one: keel first, then frames and planks added from the bottom up. *Juliet* was built from the bottom down, so to speak.

Under the direction and keen eye of Willem Alves, the aluminum-group manager, the process began with the assembly by teams of aluminum workers of three upside-down hull sections: the deck, keel and bilge. The deck sheer and beams were welded together over a long steel fixture, shaped to form the inverted sheer and deck camber. Nearby, the keel fin and ballast bulb were framed and plated. And in the center of the shed, the main portion of the underbody between frames 10 and 50 (there are 64 frames spaced 650 mm apart) was assembled on another fixture, upside-down, around it massive girders. The keel was then lifted and welded to the upside-down bilge, then that assembly was moved by cranes and set keel-up on the inverted deck, aligned and leveled by a laser, resting on a temporary steel fixture. Then the space between deck and bilge was filled in, frame by fabricated frame, stringer by stringer, until the hull form was complete. The stem plate was then added and framed, and the remaining shell plates, pre-bent to precise curvature, were fitted in and welded in place: bow to stern, sheer to bilge. In nine months, Alves and his team completed the hull, from deck to keel.

But forming a hull as lengthy as *Juliet*'s from thousands of pieces has many pitfalls, not the least of which is heat distortion. At a minimum, it can result in the occasional part having to be cajoled into place by a strong-armed worker wielding a jack, a crowbar or a hammer (one does not visit a metal-yacht building shed to meditate in silence). At its worst, heat buckles plates, shrinks the hull, alters sheer, and it can twist the hull to one side. Welding must follow a strict, symmetrical program, the key to which is the old reliable: *experience*. But Bart Bijma, Huisman's modest but inventive yard manager, does not rely solely on experience. For *Juliet*'s welding he devised a new method of heat control to reduce distortion and buckling; as a result she was welded closer to her design shape than any prior Huisman hull – her shell-plate buckling was held to an absolute minimum, thus she required far less fairing compound. Bijma's experience was also supplemented by visits from inspectors of Lloyd's Register of Shipping. This Lloyd's is not the insurance group, but a consultancy that advises shipyards on doing solid, safe work. Huisman hulls all get a "Lloyd's Certificate of Workmanship," which is given only if inspectors visit the yard often enough – at least every other week – to approve drawings, methods, materials and welds, which they regularly x-ray.

▲ *The mainsheet arch is assembled.*

▲ *Three hull sections assembled with the stem plate in place.*

Like shipbuilders everywhere, Huisman welders use MIG (Metal electrode Inert Gas) and TIG (Tungsten electrode Inert Gas) techniques, which require a constant current across a weld to make it smooth, solid and pit-free. That means a steady hand, good gear and, as the "IG" implies in both names, an inert shielding gas. Welding must be done under a shield of inert gas to prevent oxidation of the weld itself and of the material being joined, and to avoid porosity in the weld seam (recall Wolter's porous bread-like welds). The gas Huisman welders use is called Mison, a new formulation patented in 20 countries and produced by AGA Gas, a Swedish-based multinational supplier of customized gases for health care and medicine, food and beverage processing, metallurgy and packaging.

While normal shielding gases reduce atmospheric oxygen around a weld, AGA's researchers developed Mison specifically to overcome a more troublesome, more dangerous welding side effect: Ozone, or triatomic oxygen (O_3). Ozone is created by the high-energy ultraviolet light associated with the electric-arc welding process – that vibrant blue-green spark seen at electric train pantographs or sometimes in the "green flash" at sunset. While ozone is known to be a beneficent anti-greenhouse additive in the upper atmosphere, designated for protection, down here on earth where we and the welders breathe, ozone's poisonous oxidizing potential causes chest pains, headaches, breathing difficulties, watery eyes and lost work time, not to mention inferior welds. The ingredients in Mison were selected to neutralize the ozone, leaving relatively harmless byproducts and solid, strong welds.

AGA's history is filled with such salutary inventions, dating back to its founding father, Gustaf Dalén, a Swede. Dalén was a brilliant experimenter who saw profits in trying the untried, and he did extensive work to develop safe, practical and economical applications of gases. His most notable success, at the turn of the century, was the AGA Lighthouse, which embodied a remarkable self-regulating acetylene flasher, new gas-storage methods and a sun-responsive valve. The flasher became the prime night-navigation aid to the fledgling aviation industry, after being adopted worldwide as a ship navigation aid. In 1912, Dalén was awarded a contract to install AGA beacons in the lighting scheme of the yet-to-be-opened Panama Canal. That same year he was awarded the Nobel Prize in Physics.

• • •

In February 1991, when the hull was fully plated, it was hauled out into the Dutch sunshine, turned over in the arms of four gangly but powerful cranes (a frightful process to behold), set upright on a firmly welded cradle of steel and returned to the shadows of the building shed for the completion of its interior and deck welding and then to receive protective interior paint. The

▲ *Anti-buckling heat treatment.* ▼ *Grinder on temporary steps.*

▼ *Grinding a bulkhead prior to plating.*

▲ 'Twas the night before painting and the grinders were done.

oddly shimmering hull, etched with the chaotic vortex pattern of fine grinding wheels, looked like a yacht for the first time, albeit a naked, jumbo, flush-deck daysailer. Standing high above the floor, with her rounded underbody exposed, she might have reminded a visitor of the giant whale that is every New Yorker's source of wonder in the Museum of Natural History – a great leviathan smaller than a child's imagination but larger than an adult's experience. Welders soon returned to the leviathan to add the superstructure and mainsheet arch and by November 1991 she was complete externally except for her pilothouse.

During that same period she was also insulated for heat and condensation control and noise reduction. Think of a yacht's hull as a small concert hall that resonates, focuses and transmits music. But its "music" is the irksome high-decibel noise output of engines, pumps, toilets and compressors. Noise is a malediction – Arthur Schopenhauer called it the worst interruption, "a disruption of thought." In a building, noise can be tamed by mass, bulk and wide air spaces; on a sailing yacht, mass, bulk and wide spaces are anathema to comfort and performance. It takes experts to reduce shipboard noise without sinking the boat; it takes the specialist Noise & Vibration Consultancy, from Papendrecht, Holland.

A noise-reduction program must first attack the worst source, the clangorous engine room. So the consultants used sound analyses of MTU's machinery to devise this prescription: Engine and generators are set on flexible air mounts to reduce vibration into the structure; the engine room is faced with an aluminum/elastic sandwich that reflects and absorbs airborne sound; a 200-mm barrier of Rockwool, foam, lead/rubber sheeting and plywood isolates the saloon above the engine room; midships frames and stringers are bonded with a variety of foams to dampen resonances, and shell-plate faces are covered by 50 to 75 mm of an aluminum-foil/Rockwool composite that heat-insulates the hull as well, and is manufactured by the Dutch firm, Cleton Insulation. To contain the noise in the engine room and keep it from disturbing life and pleasure on deck, the intake and exhaust ventilators were given Rockwool dampers and baffles. As an important standard part of its own noise-reduction program, the yard also designs its interior construction to deaden sound and vibration: plywood floors are bonded to dense rubber so the living spaces "float" off the hull; bulkheads are nine layers of plywood, foam, lead/rubber, air and veneer to further absorb sound, and door frames have rubber seals.

The insulation was completed in early 1991 and *Juliet*'s interior was gaunt and still. Then a new, more frenetic, ritual came alive in the construction shed: An assertive army of coveralled workers from the fitting department paraded in and out and around *Juliet*'s hull. Like compulsive ants – toolboxes and

▲ *The big, bare "daysailer" is turned over.*

▲ *Framed, plated and upright, but still quite hollow.*

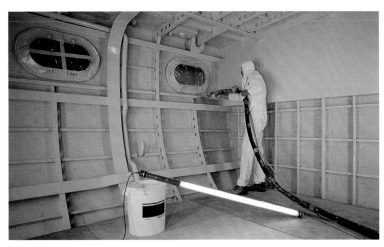

▲ *Anti-corrosive, metal-sealing paint.*

▲ *Sound-, heat-, moisture-protective foams.*

▲ *Water pipes on a stringer.* ▼ *Coiled wire, ready to conduct.*

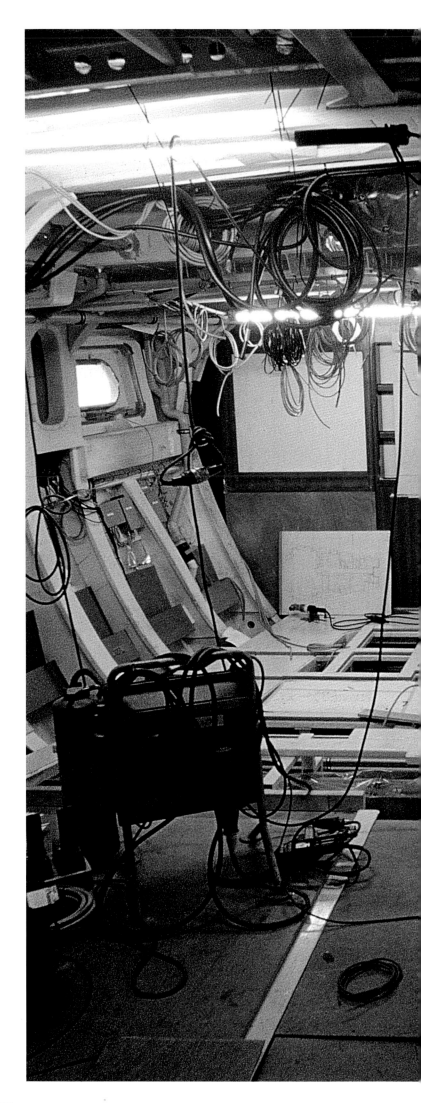

▲ *Temporary floors, lights: a masterpiece, not yet beautiful.*

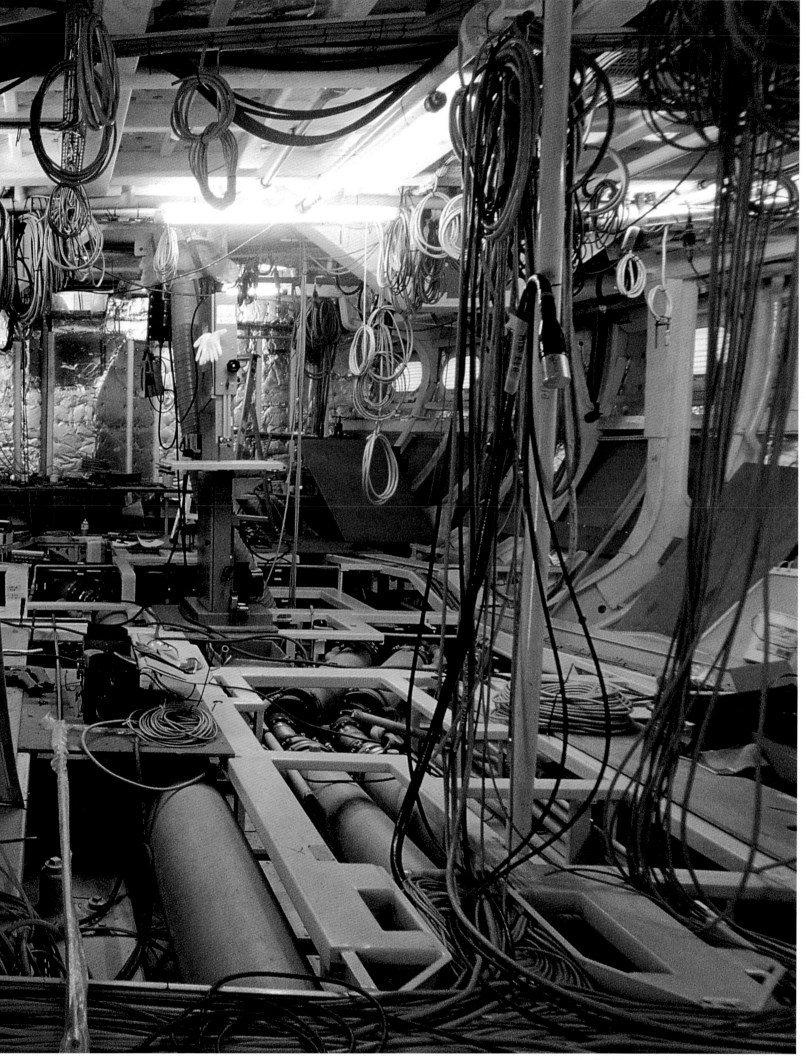

▲ *Cascades of cable await their connection.*

drawings in hand – they marched up and down the 39 aluminum steps to the scaffolding at her bow and climbed in and out of her gaping hull to install temporary plywood floors, ladders, compressors, extension cables, bright lights, ventilating fans, drill presses, saber saws and grinders. Then they began methodically installing brackets, conduits and channels under her floor beams and along her inner topsides in preparation to laying in miles of electrical cable, a refinery's-worth of plumbing, a web of pneumatic piping and 2,500 meters of hydraulic hose.

At the same time, in quiet rooms beyond the tumult of the main construction shed, workers were assembling the first rudiments of those systems, following precise schematics: junction boxes, terminal cabinets, pumps with their hoses, refrigerators with their compressors. They modified the engine, generator sets, steering motor and other machinery, adding peripherals such as hydraulic pumps and air compressors, and when ready they rolled them into the shed, raised them to the deck and lowered them into place by overhead crane.

And next door, in the shipyard storeroom, another curious process was evolving: screws, nuts, bolts, pumps, valves, elbows, pipes, nipples, springs, doorlocks, channels, tubes, insulators, connectors, cables, fuses, brackets, lamps, bulbs, sink fittings and TV sets were flowing in from suppliers, through the purchasing department into a great component library, in which each shelf was labelled *#357 – Juliet*'s hull code number. And an expendable supply of fillers, plastics, foams, grinding wheels, drill bits, caulking, tape, saw blades, sander belts and welding rod was inventoried, shelved and consumed as part of the process.

In a sense, through that period, *Juliet* grew again. But she didn't grow in length or beam (thank heavens it was too late for that!). Rather, she grew in weight and substance, as myriad items were affixed within her hollow shell, encroaching slowly into her midst, diminishing its openness by the day, shift and hour. She grew indeed as a great geode grows in a deep dark cavern by sending pure crystalline shafts of quartz toward its own center, becoming ever more compact, ever more beauteous. But at this stage *Juliet* was far from beauteous; she was more like a medical-school study model, with all the terrible secrets of her unattached organs, fluidless circulation and incomplete nervous system exposed, hanging out for everyone to work on, refine and test.

Most of that nervous system was finished in November 1991. It is all now hidden behind glorious mahogany, teak, carpeting and fine upholstery; barring disaster it will never be seen again. *Juliet* was ready to take on the first components of that glorious mahogany. But not before she was gingerly transferred from the shed for her first real beauty treatment: Fairing and painting.

● ● ●

▲ *The bare hull squeezed into the paint shed.*

Why paint an aluminum yacht? You could, after all, leave it bare and glinting in the sun, as the French are wont to do, thereby saving initial investment, expensive repainting costs and a lot of worry about scratches and scrapes. With a bare reflective hull, you might also save on air-conditioning energy and perhaps offer a better radar blip to the occasional oncoming container ship. Surely you would be welcome in La Rochelle! But a bare aluminum hull, no matter how lustrously buffed and polished, is just as vulnerable to scrapes and bangs and stains as a painted one; it still needs shielding against physical injury and a chemically hostile world. Besides, what discriminating yacht owner could possibly tolerate such a ghastly sight?

In the early 1950s the Douglas Aircraft Company faced a similar dilemma. Clients for their shiny new DC-6 liners were eager to decorate them with distinct patterns and logos. But Douglas couldn't find an appropriate paint that resisted high-speed friction, particle abrasion, hot exhausts, drastic temperature changes, fuel, cosmic and ultraviolet radiation, deicing chemicals, detergents, acid rain, mechanics' boots and Skydrol, a hydraulic oil so aggressive that when it routinely leaked from aileron controls onto wing surfaces it stripped normal paint.

The answer came from US Paint, Douglas's neighbor in St. Louis, Missouri, which distributed a German-made, 100-percent cross-linked polymer paint that resisted those elements, even the old devil Skydrol. US Paint introduced the two-part coating to the aircraft industry under the name Alumigrip and soon, in a clever marketing strategy, followed it by a similarly formulated topcoat yacht paint that also rebuffed the physical and chemical world, didn't chalk and adhered under severe pounding. Calling it first Allgrip, marketing dissidents deliberately mis-spelled it as Awlgrip to catch attention. They did.

A yacht's paint job, however, is not just a few coats of exterior paint. It is layer upon layer of diverse but compatible materials, each with a purpose to build a hard yet flexible, resistant yet attractive cosmetic cocoon. *Juliet*'s treatment, in two sessions more than a year apart, began on November 10, 1991. She was gently rolled at dawn from the shadows of the construction shed into the brilliant hospital-white fluorescence of the new paint shed. Opened in 1990, the shed is an environmentally masterful edifice that assures well-painted surfaces and healthy painters: Humidity and temperature are controlled; air is continually changed to disperse solvents; incoming air is filtered of dust that would mar painted surfaces; air is filtered on the way out in strict adherence to Dutch and European Community standards to prevent pigments and other solids from polluting the atmosphere.

The hull was first brushed with an acid-base deoxidant to clean and lightly etch the surface, making it ready to accept paint,

▲ *The rudder is faired.*

then rinsed with warm water until the surface was pH neutral. A "Mil Spec" anti-corrosive primer, then an epoxy sealing primer were applied. Then, over several days, a number of thin layers of light-weight fairing compound were trowelled on to the hull and superstructure to fill the very slight hollows left by the welding.

The fairing – a mustard-brown cement of mostly epoxy resin and tiny glass balloons blended in a great, slow-moving cake mixer – was artfully applied and smoothed over by teams using long flexible battens whose natural curvature and sawing motion progressively shaped the outer skin to perfectly match Ron Holland's lines. The surface was then meticulously sanded, and the remaining tiny voids were smoothed with a finishing filler, and sanded again. The hull was then coated with a sprayable fairing and fine-sanded once more. In all that sawing and sanding, most of the 2,400 kilos of filler trowelled on were removed, leaving a skin coating with a median thickness of only two millimeters (normally it is four, a tribute to Bart Bijma and his improved welding method).

Finally, the hull above the waterline was sprayed with one glistening Awlgrip topcoat for Huisman's master painter, Roelof van der Wetering, to check the fairing work by reflections from the surface. (Judging fairness is a matter for the eye, not the machine, proof that yacht painters are not brush-wielding automatons but true artists.)

On 1 February 1992, with Van de Wetering's blessings, *Juliet* was returned to the main shed for more interior work. But not before yardmen poured 25,500 kilos (56,000 pounds) of molten lead into her ballast bulb through the keel's side ports – a bit less than half of her total ballast, as the final weight calculations would made when machinery, furniture and appliances were installed later that year. In November 1992, after Jurrie Zandbergen did a final review of her weight calculations, the yard poured the remaining 39,500 kilos of lead into her keel to complete the ballast and trim package.

Then, in February 1993, weighing well over 200 metric tons (of which only 48.5 tons are her aluminum construction), *Juliet* was returned to the paint shed for finishing. The test topcoat was sanded off and fairing was retouched. She was again sprayed with an epoxy primer, which seals the fairing and prevents its chemical components from migrating up to the outer paint. Then, in preparation for her cosmetic topcoats – the only part of the entire paint "system" we will ever see – the painters washed the shed walls and floor with fresh water to remove dust. And the hull – now a great reservoir of static electricity owing to months of rubbing, sanding and walking traffic – was earthed (grounded) by copper wires to drain off the charge, which would ruin the spraying. Unpainted surfaces were covered by heavy paper and the

▲ *Fairing the bilge.* ▼ *Hull fairing is nearly complete.*

▼ *Fine-sanding the deckhouse.*

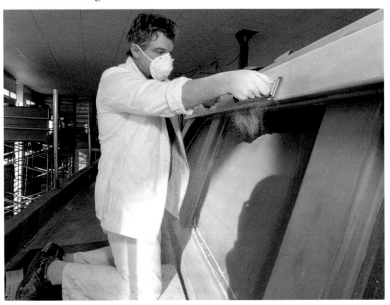

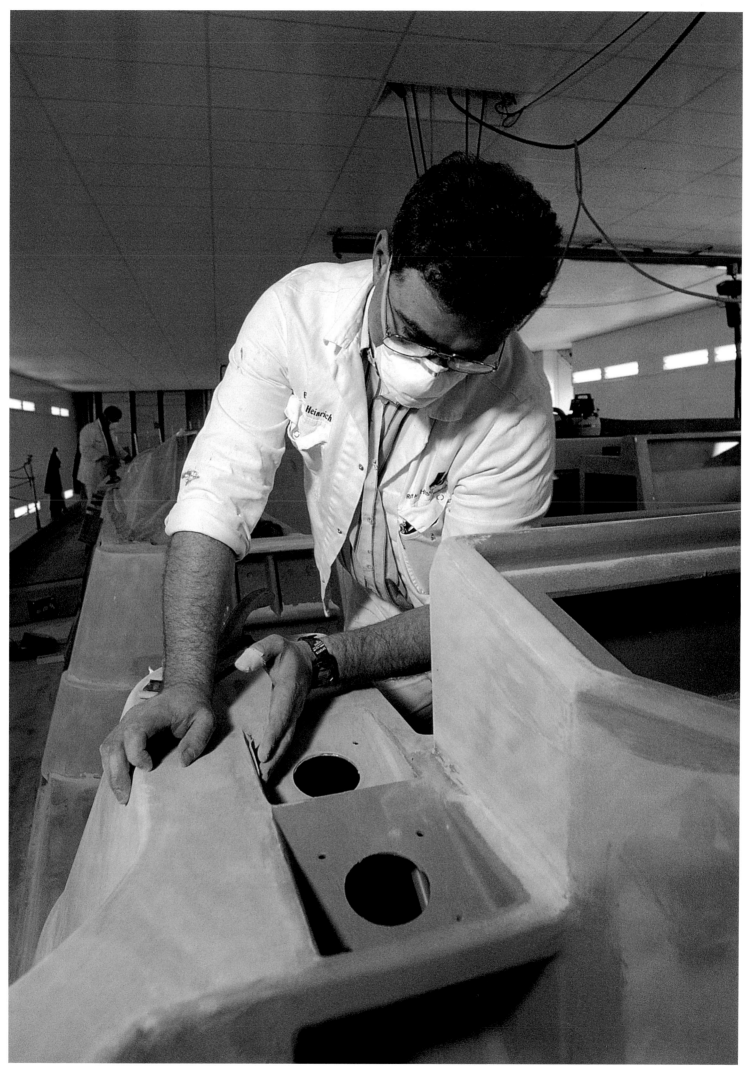

▲ *Hand-sanding the tight corners.*

hull was again surrounded by a team of masked, goggled, space-suited painters. They sprayed on two heavy topcoats, each taking about three hours to apply. They proceeded from the bow, working slowly aft on moving platforms, spraying in quick, sweeping diagonal motions to prevent paint from building up unevenly, sagging or dripping. Each coat, when it was set, was wet sanded with 2000 grit paper. Then two thinner final topcoats were applied, cautiously cross-sprayed to assure uniform thickness. It's all a bit like Chinese lacquer-work; but it's on a grand scale as *Juliet*'s paint system weighs twice what her upholstery does and three times the total of her audio and video equipment (excluding the 400 CDs).

Juliet's brilliant blue-white color comes largely from the pigment titanium dioxide. Surprisingly, much more pigment is required in white paint than in dark colors, so white paint takes somewhat longer to cure – as much as a week while the pigment settles into the base to leave clear resin on top (which is why you don't polish Awlgrip). Even after a week the paint is still stretching over the hull, reflexively becoming flatter and smoother. It is a process you can watch, if you adopt a time-lapse mentality: When *Juliet*'s last coats were sprayed on, late in the evening of February 23, 1993, her hull had an ever-so-faint orange-skin surface; in a few days of stretching it was smooth as glass and completely up to Fred Jacobs' standards.

Jacobs, a former research engineer with the Netherlands Aerospace Laboratory and now a Huisman advisor in matters technical and esoteric, regularly tests paint systems to help the yard and clients make the right choice for each project. He is concerned that every Huisman yacht passes his stringent "DOI" (Distinction Of Image) test, in which the eye of the expert or the uninitiated, roving freely over a finished hull from many angles and under many sources of harsh light, can see only clear, sharp, undistorted reflections. It was Jacobs who also selected *Juliet*'s bottom paint system: four layers of Hull Gard epoxy primer, a heavier epoxy primer and two layers of a rubber-matrix antifouling paint whose main active ingredient is biodegradable fluoric acid, which neutralizes quickly as it leeches out, and which contains no copper or tin to pollute or interact with aluminum hulls.

In late February 1993, Roelof van de Wetering's artists added the multicolored boot stripes to the waterline and painted on the elegantly scrolled name to the transom, so patiently (and repeatedly) designed by Pieter Beeldsnijder. *Juliet* was now beautified, beyond doubt. As Ivo Baeyens, Awlgrip's European vice president said when it was all done:

"It is a big collaboration to paint a yacht like *Juliet*. You need good equipment and good environmental control. But if you can't find the best painter or a guy who knows how to sand, you can't get the best result. There is no magic in a pot of paint."

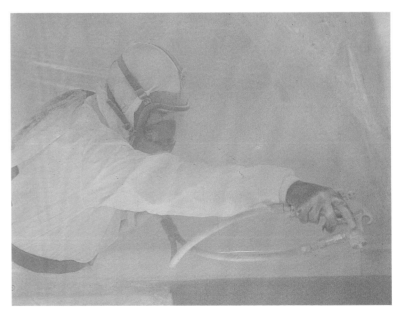

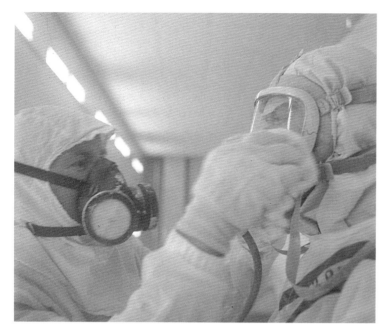

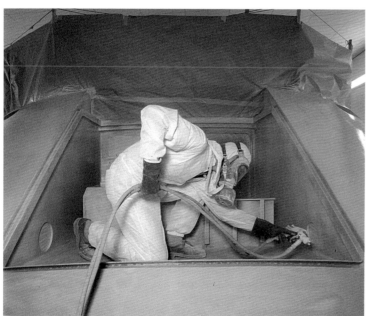

▲ *After weeks of preparation, the topcoats at last.*

RUNNING, TURNING & STANDING STILL

". . . the great engine – she never sleeps." – William Makepeace Thackeray

In 1819, two visionary Americans, Francis Fickett, a builder, and Moses Rogers, a captain, sailed the 110-foot schooner *Savannah* from her Georgia homeport to Liverpool, England, covering the 3,500 nautical miles in a slow 27 days, 11 hours. But even at that leisurely pace *Savannah* was assisted by a newfangled gadget, a paddle-wheel driven by a 90-horsepower steam engine, the first auxiliary power ever used to assist a transatlantic crossing. *Savannah*'s passage opened an era of "smelly, noisy old tea kettles" that didn't close until the turn of the century when Rudolph Diesel's internal combustor replaced the infernal boiler.

Today's sailboats no longer need colossal paddles and unsightly steam engines to gain them a few meager tenths of a knot, yet they cannot exist without serious auxiliary motive power: Despite *Juliet*'s slippery hull, tall rig and efficient sails, she will always need her engine to fill the wind's frequent voids, run her on short hops, push her into the teeth of gales, spin her around in tight harbors and power up some of her systems. It's just a fact that a megasailer's movements depend as much on Carnot's Cycle as Venturi's Effect.

For *Cyclos III*, Ron Holland selected an 890-horsepower diesel, which he set well aft, and used a "V" drive, to satisfy his client's demand for an after cockpit and a low superstructure. For *Juliet*, a very different center-cockpit boat, he set the engine amidships in the deep bilge, with a direct drive. The engine is an MTU 12V-183 TE92, an 840-hp, 12-cylinder, turbocharged, four-stroke, intercooled diesel built by Mercedes-Benz. It is adapted from the series "183" (1.83-liter cylinder volume), based on the Daimler-Benz "400" industrial series engines, thousands of which are in use in railroads, trucks and power stations.

Industrial diesels, however, are happiest when they run at high RPM, heavily loaded. On sailboats they can be very unhappy, because they are expected to run intermittently, at idle or under partial load, which invites incomplete combustion, harmful emissions and gumming up; their cooling is marginal in a constricted space; their lubrication is ineffectual at sharp angles of heel. Mercedes's marketing wing, MTU, therefore "marinizes" the diesels to optimize these factors (unlike a truck equivalent, for example, *Juliet*'s engine lubricates

properly at 23 degrees constant heel, and can tolerate somewhat deeper angles of heel for short periods).

For convenience and safety, the engine can be started from the steering pedestals, pilothouse or engine room, and as soon as the engine starts, engine-room ventilator fans start as well. An emergency starter in the forepeak and an engine-driven hydraulic pump driving the capstan allow the crew to re-anchor in case they drag, without having to run 105 feet aft to the cockpit. Engine exhaust gases run through some 27 meters of eight-inch cupronickel piping, cooled by raw water circulating through sections of flex-mounted polypropylene jacket. This holds down back pressure and eliminates the need for bulky insulation. So much depends on the raw-water manifold, which supplies cooling water to engine, generators, exhausts, gearbox, hydraulic pumps and propeller shaft, that the supply is monitored by a flow indicator and temperature alarms; and if the main pumps fail, the deckwash pump can be pulled into service to replace it. The 20,850 liters (5,500 US gallons) of diesel fuel are stored in five tanks under the floors and in the keel fin. Fuel, transferred to a day tank through a cartridge-type separator, is also cooled by some of that raw water, as MTU recommends it be injected at 20° C to assure that the engine develops full rated power. And since all this hot machinery also needs lubrication, some 250 liters of oil are distributed among the engine, generators and a reservoir.

The diesel drives the boat through a ZF 4:1-reduction gearbox, which is flex-coupled to a long shaft that terminates in the hub of a variable-pitch propeller, about seven meters from the engine coupling. The propeller is a product of Hundested, the renowned Danish company that has made propulsion systems for fishing vessels, cargo ships, tugs, ferries, high-speed patrol boats and yachts since 1929. Hundested's rationale for its brand of "Multi Pitch" propellers is straightforward: a fixed propeller designed for high speed can't deliver good low-speed power; a fixed propeller designed for low-speed power can't deliver good top-end speed. A propeller whose pitch is continuously changeable over a wide range, however, can do all those things and more: It can be pitch-adjusted to deliver speed over

◀ *MTU diesel: painted and ready.*

▲ *Port transom exhaust is installed.* ▼ *Engine "doctors" check the monitoring system.*

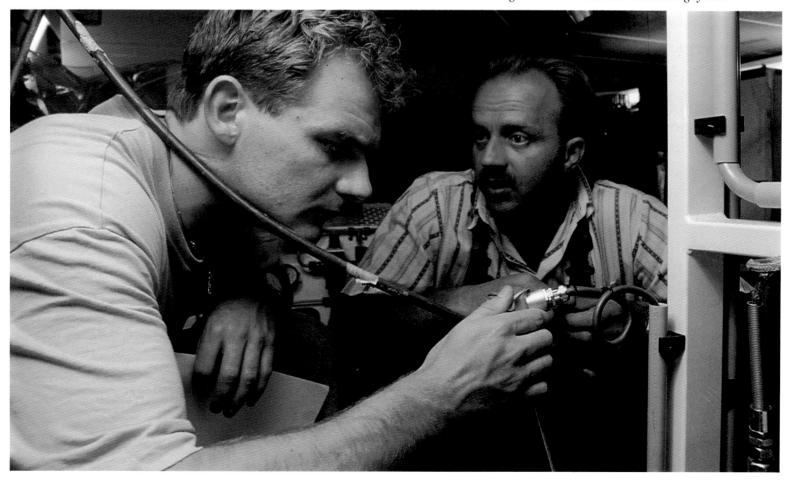

the long haul or power for maneuvring; the pitch can be adjusted to improve fuel economy as measured by engine exhaust temperature; when the boat is motorsailing, the pitch can be tuned to the wind-driven speed to reduce drag; under sail alone the propeller blades can be feathered to reduce resistance, and a damaged blade can easily be replaced.

The Multi Pitch prop Hundested selected for *Juliet* is a VP-9^1/$_2$, a 1400-mm (55-inch) four-bladed masterwork crafted from nickel-aluminum bronze, whose efficiency and sculptural beauty would make Captain Nemo proud (indeed, this prop is modelled after those Hundested designed for silent-running submarines, with swept-back blades to reduce vibration and concentrate thrust). To allow the pitch to be varied continuously, the blades pivot around bearings, turned by a rod that translates within the hollow shaft, and which is moved by an electric motor, through gearing. Designed by a proprietary Hundested computer program, the prop is large enough to push *Juliet*'s fully-loaded 260-ton hull at better than 13 knots, yet turn slowly enough to minimize cavitation (the undesirable vacuum effect that reduces propeller efficiency and harms blades).

All couplings, also designed by computer program, are made of rubber that is formulated to be soft enough to dampen vibration, but hard enough to transmit power without harmful backlash. All the couplings, shaft bearings, the Exalto-brand shaft seals and the isolated stainless-steel strut that supports the shaft outside the hull also serve to totally dissociate the big bronze propeller from the aluminum hull to prevent electrolytic interaction in sea water.

▲ *Hundested's Multi Pitch bronze sculpture.*

▲ *The mighty MTU diesel engine in its permanent home.*

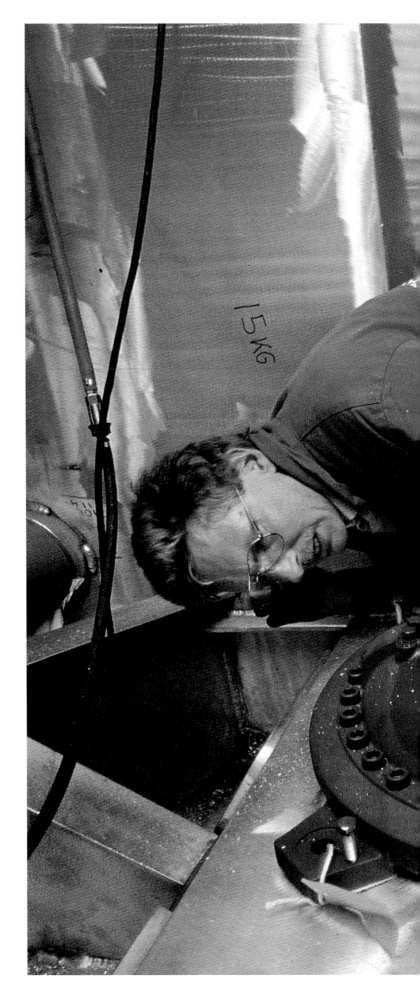

It takes all of this just to move *Juliet* forward and backward. But what about moving her sideways? Pushing a 260-ton object with lots of windage off a dock, when there is a beam-on gale blowing it back on the dock, cannot be done without powerful help. For that *Juliet* has Hundested bow and stern thrusters. The two 85-horsepower units – hinged to swing down for deployment, but faired perfectly into the hull when retracted – assure the crew they can "claw off" a lee dock in as much as Force Seven winds (28 to 33 knots). This was proven during sea trials in Den Helder when she slipped off rather handily in that breeze, with higher gusts and 80 people aboard. Like all her hydraulic gear, the thrusters are proportionally controlled: the more joystick, the higher the propeller RPM. And just two fingers do all the work.

• • •

That is how *Juliet* moves, either in a straight line or sideways. What about steering her off the straight and narrow? Well, anyone who has sailed a dinghy knows what steering is all about: Tiller in one hand, mainsheet in the other, jibsheet between teeth, centerboard pennant around a big toe, you react to changing wind and water forces by "feel" to maintain heel angle, heading and speed; it is a visceral application of Norbert Wiener's favorite hobby, *feedback*. But coaxing a 260-ton yacht across an ocean or into a small bay is a bit different. You can't hope to counter forces with teeth and toes; you need high mechanical advantage. You still need the "feel," but it must come through some sort of power-leveraging mechanism, which is why cables and quadrants, blocks and tackles, servomechanisms, chain drives, worm gears, electromagnets, universal-jointed rods, rack-and-pinions, giant wheels, lengthy tillers and muscular helmsmen have found their way into marine steering systems.

The special qualities of *Juliet*'s steering came out of the owner's unflinching demand for lightness at the helm within the enormous power required to bridle her weight and her 3.5-meter rudder (one-third of a sailboat's side force comes from the rudder and skeg, and at heavy-weather reaching speeds that is a force to reckon with). During meetings, several steering systems – quadrant and rods in particular – were considered and rejected in favor of the proven power and reliability of hydraulics. But the client disdains a typical hydraulic helm's insensitivity and non-linearity; he pleaded for the team to find some clever *new* means for the helmsman to feel the wind and sea through the wheel. When he showed them a highly sensitive hydraulic-caliper bicycle brake, Wolter and his systems designers, Jan Bokxem and Jurrie Zandbergen, were inspired to try an idea they had toyed with before: They set out to reinvent the wheel – or the *tiller*, as it turned out.

Under sail, *Juliet* is indeed steered by a "tiller," a meter-long lever mounted on her rudder post. The tiller is controlled by a

▲ *Steering "muscle," the Tjenford hydraulic motor.*

▲ *Captain Kiendl fingertip-steers by Robertson autopilot.*

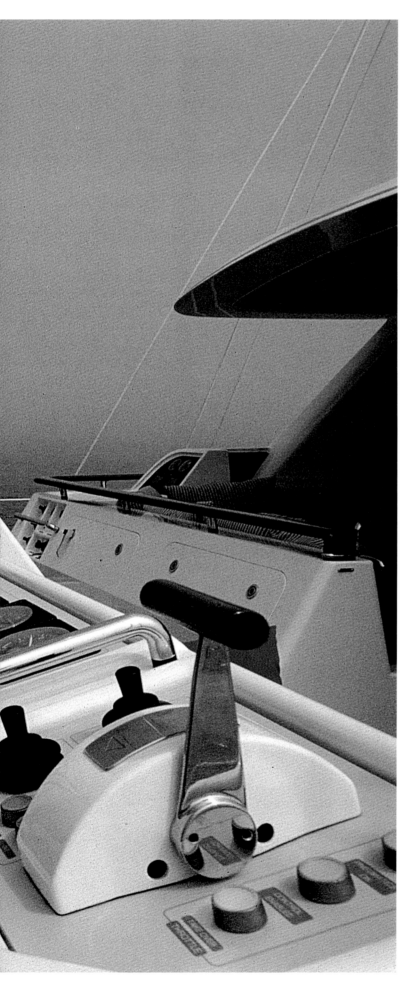

closed-loop static hydraulic system of enormous power and sensitivity. When either wheel is engaged and turned, a chain-and-sprocket drive moves a rack fixed to a hydraulic ram under the cockpit. That ram's cylinder is coupled by dual hydraulic hoses to an identical cylinder linked to the "tiller." Movement of the forward ram is replicated by the rudder ram, which pivots the tiller and turns the rudder proportionally.

By its symmetry, the steering also feeds some rudder torque back to the wheel, so the helm has a degree of "feel" befitting the weather conditions, important in maximizing performance and giving the helmsman a damned good time. Helm sensitivity is enhanced by low-friction seals in the cylinders. For optimum performance, however, the Hydraudyne seals need to operate at a base pressure of 30 bar (about 30 atmospheres), provided by a small pump. Under steering load, of course, cylinder pressures rise, and will reach 200 bar or more with heavy weather helm. Should it approach a very unlikely 400 bar, as a safety the cylinder bodies will distort, relieving the load. A cylinder may be ruined, but it is replaceable (which is more than one can say about the one and only rudder).

If conditions get that heavy, and hand steering is too difficult, or *Juliet* embarks on a long passage under the guidance of her autopilot, the crew can turn on the real "power steering," a powerful Tjenford hydraulic motor. The motor, set astride the rudder post, is fingertip-controlled by joysticks at the pedestals, pilothouse or crow's nest, or it is commanded by her autopilot program. Activating the power system and shifting steering away from the wheels takes only the touch of a button on one of the autopilot units: Then the rudder-motor clutch closes on the rudder post, the motor is powered up hydraulically and both wheels are uncoupled, spinning free to prevent anyone getting caught and hurt in their spokes. The autopilot that is the heart of this operation is a Robertson AP9 MKII, a rugged, versatile, widely used device, winner of the NMEA's 1993 "Best Autopilot" award, and installed by Bennex, the Dutch wing of the Norwegian company that developed it, Robertson Tritech.

A modern autopilot is a uncanny device: Through a few elegant circuits it holds a steadier heading than the best helmsman, executes perfect turns, counters weather helm and will find a waypoint without asking any questions except where it and the waypoint are (all without complaint or consuming food). The AP9 MKII does it all with three circuit boards. It not only steers automatically, but is adjustable to meet sailing conditions and each vessel's characteristic motion. At its best, with all accessories on line, the Robertson AP9 is capable of holding, say, oil-rig supply boats, survey ships and rescue boats in a stationary position by balancing their props, rudders and thrusters regardless of wind,

wave and current. The Huisman yard installed such a dynamic-positioning system on the 112-foot *Acharné*, but on *Juliet* it was thought unnecessary, so the Robertson is used primarily for intelligent steering and, in conjunction with the Plath gyrocompass, Trimble Loran/Satnav and Chart Plotter, some quite sophisticated automatic navigation.

From sailing under autopilot, the steering can again be transferred to the wheels at the touch of a button: the rudder motor dis-clutches and the wheels re-clutch. This switching back and forth between systems has only one small drawback: Any time steering is transferred from wheel to autopilot, the rudder motor's angular position will almost surely not coincide with the true rudder position. But it must, or the motor will not have equal throw on either side, limiting the steering flexibility, which is unsafe. So, when the switch is made from the wheel back to powered steering, the feedback of the Robertson autopilot quickly compares the rudder motor position to the rudder lever angle, turns the motor to the correct alignment and then re-clutches the motor. Those dry sailors thought of everything.

But maybe too much. Though the steering has redundancy and safety built in, with alarms for electrical or hydraulic failure, as it is an entirely new system almost everyone had some small doubts about it. Early on, when no one knew whether any of it would work, the client mused: "I once thought a fifty footer was huge; how could I drive a boat this big? It's a

staggering object." Ron Holland thought that the yard was over-extending itself in designing these new systems; he felt comfortable with existing technologies. And Wolter, explaining the closed-loop hydraulics to a visitor concluded: "I hope it's going to work. Everybody was against me, but I have been sailing for so many years, and I know that you don't *steer* a boat, you *feel* a boat." (Wolter did worry, in fact, that the two wheel-steering hydraulic cylinders, which must always be in identical positions for the steering to function, might over a period of time slip out of phase, limiting rudder angle on one side. So he prescribed a method of recalibration, just in case. And it is well that he did. On *Juliet*'s maiden transatlantic passage a slight mis-adjustment did occur, and in Bermuda her engineer quickly adjusted it, and learned to avoid it in the future.)

Perhaps the greatest sources of concern were the system's sophistication and its potential to generate crew complacency. One of its principle designers, Jan Bokxem, had plenty of time to consider that troubling aspect during the building process. A designer with more than usual skill in solving mechanical problems, and more than the usual intuition about the risks associated with the hyper-mechanical life, once said of the system: "It's really idiot-proof. Except for that rare idiot. But we think sailing must still be a challenge; we must allow the crew to do things; we don't want the crew to stay on shore while the boat goes out under electronic control. Sailing still must be fun."

▲ *Navigation: yesterday and today.*

THE BODY ELECTRIC

"You shall have joy, or you shall have power, said God; you shall not have both." – Ralph Waldo Emerson

In July 1974 a 43-foot ocean racer named *Circe* was motoring out of Hamilton Harbour after finishing the Bermuda Race when her engine suddenly seized a shaft bearing. Sailing to St. Georges, the crew was informed by a local mechanic that he would have no problem replacing the bearing. *In six weeks.* They set sail for New York. On that 650-mile voyage, unable to charge the batteries, the crew learned just how much a 43-foot ocean racer depends on electricity: They had to rig emergency navigation and binnacle lights, use flashlights below, keep radio silent, use the Loran sparingly, dead-reckon diligently, pump water and bilges by hand, use the portable direction finder, drink warm juice and eat cold sandwiches. When they arrived home on the flood tide they stopped *Circe*'s thirteen tons smartly at the yacht club dock by backing her mainsail. It was a feat of rather ordinary seamanship, and the batteries were still nearly full.

But what of *Juliet*'s need for electricity? She is three and one-third times longer, twenty times heavier and has a hundred times more lights: Can her electrical needs compare with a 43-footer's? Can it be reduced without impairing pleasure, convenience or safety? Can any 143-foot sailboat even move without electric power? The answers are *no, no* and, well, *maybe.* Everything aboard a large yacht consumes power: refrigeration, heating, ice making, air conditioning, electronics, lights, furlers, winches, thrusters, capstan, vacuum, washers, pumps, audio and tools; so does the cook microwaving a single cup of cocoa or rustling up a gourmet meal for twelve; or a guest watching a video, flushing a toilet or telephoning home. Behind every one of these functions there are batteries, which start generators, which activate chargers that replenish batteries – an endless power cycle in which hundreds of gadgets and gizmos are drawing off their just portion of power, all for the good life.

This almost lurid truism once prompted the client (who honestly dreamed of a "battery boat") to liken *Juliet* to a certain American fast-food chain: "From opening day," he said, "a Dunkin' Donuts never closes; unless it burns down it makes donuts 24 hours a day, forever." *Juliet*, too, will "make donuts" 24 hours a day. Forever. Using electricity.

To begin with, she is an "international" boat using 50-Hz alternating current (AC), produced by three paralleled, synchronized, phased MTU-diesel-driven generators made by Leroy Somer (no *known* relation to the author): One generator is rated at 15 kW and two at 60 kW. The generators staunchly crank out 380-volt, 50-Hz AC into a three-phase grid. The main bus bar for heavy gear – compressors, pumps, boilers and hydraulic power packs – taps off the full 380 volts; another bus for amusements, galley and some communications equipment taps off 220 volts; a good portion of those 220-volt house needs are also served by a circuit supplied by inverters when the generators are off, and another bus is energized by separate inverters that circulate 110-volt *60-Hz* AC for Macintosh computers and suchlike. For direct current (DC) consumers, such as navigation and sailing instruments, radios and lights, yet another bus takes 24 volts directly off the batteries or from 380-volt lighting transformers when the generators are running. And a small transformed 12-volt bus bar is used to re-charge portable batteries for hand-held gear such as lamps and tools.

Any attempt to *manually* manage such a formidable mix of AC and DC enterprises, with five voltages, two frequencies, two waveforms and a host of alternate sources, would clearly be folly. So the Dutch power specialists, R&H Technology, designed an automated power-management system to allow the engineer an occasional coffee break or a night's sleep. The R&H system fills five large engine room panels: three each contain a "620" computer that monitors and alarms one of the generators; one contains the shore-power monitor, and the last contains a "Ricom 2000," a central processor that, like HAL in "2001: A Space Odyssey," has a higher intelligence. The 2000 inter-manages and monitors the generators and the entire onboard matrix of power and security systems, from exhausts in the lazarette, to batteries amidships, to clothes washer in the forepeak, to opening ports everywhere. The 2000 directs power sharing of all onboard consumers; it identifies hundreds of problems as they develop, sets off warning alarms and shuts down machinery if necessary. And it displays for the engineer a full record of events,

◀ *Wire, wire, everywere ....*

readings and alarms on a monitor screen in the engine room, or on repeaters in the crew mess and at the helm stations.

Primarily designed to save fuel, the 2000 continually measures the power demand of all consumers and activates the right combination of generators needed to meet the demand, thus guarding them against overload and under-use. Say, the 15-kW generator is running and a crew, cleaning up after dinner, turns the dishwasher on, which raises demand above 90 percent of the generator's capacity. Automatically (and in seconds), one standby 60-kW generator is started and joins the 15-kW generator on line; then the washer is supplied with current and allowed to start. If other consumers are switched on and demand exceeds 90 percent of that generator's capacity, the other big one comes on line. If there is a very large power drain, as when several hydraulic winches are in use, the 2000 shuts down as many low-priority consumers as necessary to keep demand below available power. (Priorities are assigned to some 100 consumer groups: deckwash pumps and stereos have low priority; bilge pumps higher; watermakers, sheet winches and furling gear still higher; steering hydraulics, fuel pumps, battery chargers and engine ventilators have top priority and never shut down.)

Or take the actual case when, during her sea trials, *Juliet* was maneuvered alongside a windblown quay, with the captain using thrusters and the crew using deck winches to overhaul lines. One 60-kW generator was running. When the captain initiated bow and stern thrusters, the 2000 started the 15-kW generator and dumped the "house" load onto it. Then it started the other 60-kW generator and both big diesels, which normally run at 1,500 RPM to generate 50-Hz current, revved up to 2,200 RPM to deliver their full power to the hydraulic thruster pumps (all this in about fifteen seconds). When the boat was secure alongside and thrusters were retracted, the 2000 shut down one 60-kW generator, shifted the house load back to the other, and shut down the 15-kW generator, returning the system to its prior condition. Finally, when a shore-

▲ *An R&H technician oversees the Ricom 2000.*

Juliet

▲ *Circuit makers, circuit breakers … by the thousands.*

▲ *One corner of the battery installation.*

power connection was made, the 2000 shut down the remaining 60-kW generator for silent operation. (Should shore power be interrupted, however, a generator would be started again.)

The Ricom 2000 makes an astonishing mix of observations and decisions. But it is not totally independent. As one R&H technician said: "With all this automation it would seem that ships no longer need an engineer. But you must have an engineer to manage the power management, despite the automation. The engineer must be part of the system." The price the engineer pays to be part of the system is taking time to learn a great many codes, being wakened from that occasional night's sleep by an alarm (real or false) and having to consort with a 146-page manual whose trouble-shooting instructions begin calmly, but ever so ominously: *DON'T PANIC.*

• • •

Inasmuch as the AC and DC power distribution and management require heavy cables and medium wires, and scores of fine signal lines from each consumer to the Ricom computer, this electrical microcosm had to be wired by someone before it could be expected to power-manage one cup of cocoa, let alone a gourmet meal for twelve. The responsibility for that, and for all of *Juliet*'s interlocking circuits, fell to Jack Corbeek, manager of the electrical department. Corbeek, at Huisman since the late 1970s, has the intellect and inner calm needed to master such a maze of wires, voltages, currents and consumers: He was in radio and television and is a former Siemens engineer; he runs a home-built studio where he records Dutch gospel music, and to find silence and clean air he climbs mountains (but surely not in Holland). Corbeek drew schematics for all the electrical systems and prescribed components, interfaces and connectors to create a corrosion-free, shock-resistant, completely-hidden network. In doing so he wired 260 spotlights, more than 50 lamps, 43 light dimmers and 283 meters of tube and strip lights that run hidden along furniture bases and in overheads. If you exclude all equipment pilot lamps and the crew's pocket flashlights, that amounts to

▲ *Double, double coil and trouble . . . .*

5,729 separate light bulbs on board this former "battery boat." And that's just the lighting! All together, Corbeek and his electricians installed 47 kilometers of wire (two and a half times the length of Manhattan) weighing 12,500 kilos (about the same as a Dutch-built, heavy-displacement Hutting 40 sloop), more than a thousand 24-volt fuses and as many magnetohydrodynamic circuit-breakers (made in Switzerland by Heinemann).

To orchestrate this wiring fugue, Corbeek had to first set terminal boxes in strategic places. These enclosures, though, are not just bent-metal cabinets; they are of a patented design by Rittal BV, a major ship supplier. One wouldn't think so, but yacht wiring is subject to worse conditions than industrial plant wiring; Rittal cabinets are designed to resist moisture, salt and vibration, which wreak havoc with electrical systems. They are particularly important on *Juliet*, because they are chock-full of the thousands of terminals, connectors and interfaces that keep all that current flowing in the right direction and to the right consumers, and which are made by Rittal's sister company, Phoenix Contact BV, a part of Cito Benelux, a multinational firm that built its reputation supplying electric components to the petrochemical industry.

The Phoenix Contact connectors are not just made up from screws and threaded plates on bases; those would corrode or shake loose in no time. They have nickel-plated copper terminals and copper screws, whose similar expansion rate in the heat of current flow keeps them from loosening. The contacts are of more than a dozen designs, each dedicated to large or small wire, solid or stranded wire, high or low current, ganging of connectors or quick removal. And many are set in delicious green polyamide housings, in swing-out racks for easy servicing. There are, in fact, 4,134 such Phoenix terminals in those Rittal cabinets, each holding one wire, or joining two or three, the other ends of which pop up at a light switch, a pump or a juice squeezer. And when there is something electronic and sensitive at the other end – radar, computer, chart plotter or sailing instrument – there are 250 interface connections made by Phoenix Optocouplers, which transmit signals between light-emitting diodes and light-sensitive transistors so there is no mechanical connection to invite interference or galvanic action.

▲ *But, are they connected to anything?*

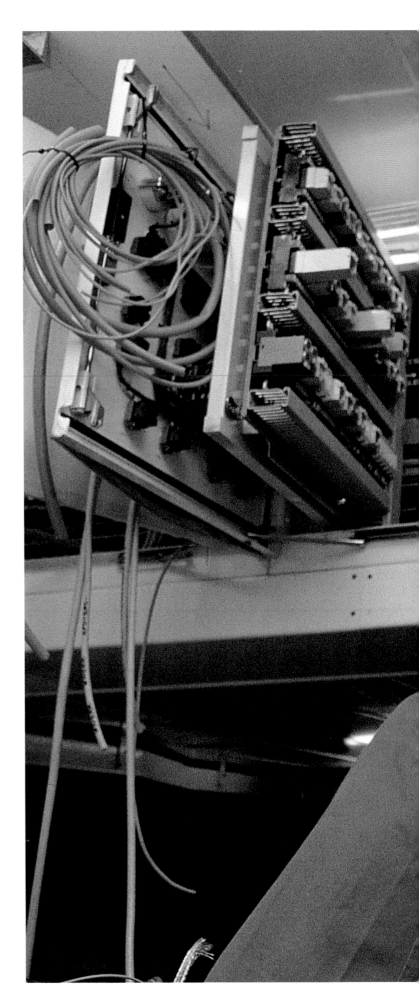

▲ *"Who drew this schematic?"*

After all that physical wiring, Corbeek and his crew had to check that both the ends of every wire were connected to their proper recipient and that current flowed through every one of those 47 kilometers, which they did with meters and steady hands. The next time you rewire an old lamp, think of Jack Corbeek.

• ● •

There is a gentle bay on the mainland of Scotland opposite the isle of Mull called Eilean Nam Beathach, more commonly Puilldobhrain. Under ideal conditions – late of a midsummer evening, in light airs and in a bit of Scottish mist – this place is Tranquility Base on Earth. Only cuckoos, doves and the lapping of the tide can be heard, and no yachtsman would dare enter this heaven-sent anchorage with music blaring or generators churning. In such circumstance, surely, *Juliet*'s owner and crew would shut all generators down. The moment they do more circuits take over to assure the good (quiet) life, and begin drawing down the 3,000 amp-hours of current stored in 24 sealed, gel-filled Sonnenschein batteries, from Atsa Batterijen in Holland. The gel-type battery is ideal for large sailboats: it is invulnerable to heeling and needs little maintenance. But gel batteries are not free of care: they produce gas if overcharged and cannot be allowed to run down too much. They must be topped off properly, for which *Juliet* has four battery chargers that adjust the charge rate according to voltage levels, power demand and ambient temperature.

The chargers were developed by Victron Energie, whose parent, Victron BV, pioneered inverter and power supply technology and uninterruptible power sources for computers. Victron was founded in 1975 by a young physics student, Reinout Vader, who saw a need for fail-safe energy sources under the adverse conditions onboard ships. He developed tailored systems for commercial and fishing vessels, police launches and lifeboats, and thousands of European canal and river boats. More recently Victron has made similar portable systems for campers, mobile libraries, x-ray buses, and homes and businesses in areas with irregular power sources.

It is irregular power sources that required installation of several Victron Energie inverters under *Juliet*'s floors. Fresh water

▲ *"Where is that schematic?"*

▲ *The Ricom (right); engineer Steve Laing (left).*

pumps, toilets, freezers, refrigerators are on call at any time, whether the generators are running or not. When generators are running, they are powered off the normal 220-volt bus; when the generators are shut down, they must get their power from inverters, which take 24-volt DC off the batteries and step it up (producing only the gentlest of hums) to 220-volt 50-Hz AC. These inverters, however, create a less-critical *trapezoidal* waveform that can be used by motor-driven devices. For more sensitive Macintosh computers, or hair dryers, shavers and other American gadgets, all of which use 60-Hz current, two more Victron Energie inverters supply the guest cabins with 110-volt 60-Hz *sinusoidal* AC.

Even with inverter power available, there will be times at anchor when the boat needs the power of generators, so silencing them was a top design priority. The 15-kW "night" generator is enclosed by a sound-shielding box and all three are set on pneumatic bases with inflating side mounts that support them when the boat heels. Their exhausts, like the main engine's, are silenced and water-jacketed. To avoid the smell and soot of effluent when guests are swimming off the stern, the 15-kW and port-side 60-kW generators exhausts combine to exit amidships at the waterline. But, once the boat gets under way, they should properly exhaust astern, so as the engine is started and the gearbox is engaged (or if sail is set and *Juliet* heels five degrees) the Ricom 2000 resets pneumatic valves, shunts the exhausts to the transom and seals the side outlet to prevent water entering the exhaust system.

With 135 kilowatts of generator power, added inverter power, 3,000 amp-hours of battery power and more than 20,000 liters of fuel to energize them all, *Juliet* has power to spare. But she will need it: In her galley alone there are: microwave and hot-air ovens, coffee and espresso makers, juice extractor, grill, ice-cube maker, hood ventilator, garbage disposal, trash compactor, dishwasher, audio/video center, 1,300 liters of freezer capacity and 1,175 liters of refrigerator. Most of these get used every day. And the cook also has a very large capacity cake-batter mixer, in case she has to mix up a batch of her very best donuts. Wouldn't those old-time, donut-loving, seat-of-the-pants sailors on *Circe* love an invitation for a sail on *Juliet*!

▲ *Soft lights, sweet music ...*

▲ *... when every wire is in the right place.*

AIR, EARTH, WATER & FIRE

There are moments when everything goes well; don't be frightened, it won't last." – Jules Renard

"Forewarned forearmed." – Miguel de Cervantes

A boat is like a home: When there's water in the basement, you want to find its source. So *Juliet* has an exhaustive monitoring and alarm system built into the Ricom computer to protect her against misadventures, malfunctions and security lapses. As most of these functions are out of sight and hearing of the crew, they have to be watched constantly (during sea trials they were watched so constantly by the nervous computer that, until it was fine tuned, it set off lots of alarms, one assumes, just to be on the safe side). The computer in fact monitors nearly 400 nominal functions. For example, it sounds an alarm when temperature, pressure and flow rate of cooling water, lubricating oil and compressed air fall outside the required ranges; it warns of low fuel or water tanks, or tanks that are filled with dirty fuel or impure water, or sumps ready for pumping out; it warns of overheated batteries, under-cooled freezers, an overburdened generator, an under-deployed thruster or a failed ice-cube maker. It will shout when the total house current demand reaches 400 amps. The five bilge sections, as another example, have redundant pumps, but if a

pump fails or a bilge over-fills the alarm is sounded. Or if one of the 17 opening portlights is left open – inviting a thief in harbor or seawater under way – a microswitch sounds the alarm and identifies the open port on the monitor screens. The gangway and passarelle have bells for welcome guests to announce themselves; a pressure-sensitive doormat announces them, welcome or not, and several mini-cameras deliver clear color images of them below.

Surely the most crucial monitor aboard any yacht is for that most nightmarish of emergencies: a fire below. The yard team led by project manager Jan Bokxem fully analyzed the question, to structure a system that gives the crew every advantage in dousing a fire, without risky delay, without confusion. There are smoke alarms in key points in the accommodation area, and smoke and heat detectors in the engine room and lazarette. The galley, a singularly fire-prone place, has a special system to combat its worst-case situation – a grease fire. Most galley fires can be doused by CO_2, Halon or a fireproof blanket. But if grease is enflamed, it must be denied oxygen to halt the flame and, more important,

▲ *Setting up galley ventilation and firefighting.*

cooled to prevent its re-igniting. Firefighting materials such as Halon or CO_2, however, do not cool grease, and by replacing oxygen they endanger occupants who are fighting the fire. So the yard installed a cartridge-pressurized tank of soapy water over the gas range, activated by high heat, which will instantly disgorge its contents over all burners and harmlessly douse any flame.

In case of fire in the engine room, an alarm bell sounds and lights flash there. While most other alarms aboard can be bypassed by an "accept" button, the fire alarm cannot be turned off for five minutes, to assure a response. Nor is there an automatic firefighting sequence: The crew must enter the engine room to assess the nature and extent of the fire before releasing the Halon. Then they have two choices: One is to shut down the generators and cut their fuel off, at which time the engine-room ventilator fans also stop, to reduce the air supply. For safety, however, the engine does not shut down. This allows the crew to move the boat away from other boats, or to a lee to prevent wind from further exciting the flames; and it allows time for them to analyze their situation and measure the consequences of their actions. Because, if they elect the second choice, and activate the Halon, the engine-room ventilators are sealed and the engine is stopped – they can no longer maneuver. Trying to second-guess a crew under the strain of a fire was no easy task. "This was the source of much heated discussion," Jan Bokxem recalls, with surely no pun intended. "In order to fight fire properly, you must think before you act!"

● ● ●

Thomas Mann wrote: "The word, even the most contradictory word, preserves contact – it is silence which isolates." Perhaps that is all the justification needed for *Juliet*'s 20 telephone handsets, cordless and cellular phones. From any set one can pass the word over the PA system or to a set at the other end of the boat. To reach a set at the other end of the world the caller can use a land line (when at dockside), a cellular hookup (when in range of a relay station) or the SatCom "A," which uses a satellite network. For transmitting the word by radio, the boat has two Skanti VHF transceivers and six control units, with antennas atop the main and mizzen masts that give ship-to-ship and ship-to-shore ranges beyond the usual 50 miles; a 750-watt Skanti single-side band transceiver is used for worldwide communication. The SatCom, cellular and land-line hookups are all compatible with the facsimile, computers and telephones for every imaginable form of communication, from fax, to "E" mail, to just calling home.

Many of these devices reside snugly in the navigation room, a work of mahogany-and-electronic art. Seated at one of its two swivel chairs one can use the facsimile/printer, VHF transceiver, cellular phone, SatCom keyboard and monitor, Furuno radar with ARPA collision-avoidance, chart navigator, Macintosh and Compaq computers, a 20" Sony TV and computer monitor and an Alden weather fax. Or one can sit back and view the Trimble Loran-GPS, Meteostar barograph, Plath gyrocompass, Brookes & Gatehouse sailing instruments and even slide a pair of dividers, parallels and pencils over a paper chart. Or just by stretching a bit

▲ *Monitoring the master monitor.*

one can pull down one of the nearly 60 technical manuals that line the shelves. With the yard's zealous aid, this electromagnetic kingdom was installed by the navigation electronics specialist Sailtron, of Utrecht. And no easy task it was. Practically everything onboard and in the room interfaces with practically everything else: SatCom and gyro; gyro and autopilot; autopilot and chart navigator; true-motion radar and autopilot — only the espresso-maker seems to have been left out on its own. To quote one of the expert installers: "The interfacing was only a bottleneck, but the shielding was a nightmare!" But, then, it takes dreams to have nightmares.

• ● •

The installation of the audiovisual centers, by Ehringa Media, of Groningen, was also a major electronic challenge. The television network (the appropriate name for it) consists of one VHS and three video-8 players and six television sets. Guests can watch tapes, broadcasts or home-grown videos shot aboard with portable cameras (reliving yesterday's rack of scudding clouds while eating today's rack of delicious lamb). A film or video can be punched up on any set, which can monitor security cameras or display the electronic chart so guests can see where they are without pestering the navigator. A video editing and sound mixing console allows more adventuresome filming. And with the Roland electric piano and its thousands of timbres and rhythms, if there's a good piano player aboard, she certainly can be commandeered into playing background melodies to any private video showing.

• ● •

If you lift the starboard helm seat you will find an odd maze of gray-metal tubes resembling an architect's model of an oil refinery; it is the nexus of pneumatic controls for engine throttle and gearbox, a critical link in *Juliet*'s life under power. Long cable controls are too cumbersome, hard to maintain and friction-plagued, so the designers choose to remotely control all machinery by compressed air (recognized by the characteristic little "sneeze" as the throttle hits neutral). They mounted the main air compressor on the back of the engine so that while it runs it fills four tanks through pressure-sensitive valves, providing pressure at the cockpit and pilothouse helm stations (and through circuitry to the crow's nest), with enough left to run air-operated tools, fill generator mounts, sound the horn and open and close exhaust valves. A second, 380-volt, compressor kicks in when the pressure falls short of demand.

For air with quite a different purpose, there is a central vacuum cleaner in the engine room and piping leading to nine outlets spread throughout the boat so the crew can vacuum-clean the entire house, toting only a hose and cleaning head, plugging it in where needed. The vacuum piping, under the floors, has transparent elbows wherever it bends so blockages can be spotted and cleared by a custom-designed tool. Another air-based system with somewhat more imperative purpose is the heating. In cold weather the interior is warmed by blowers forcing air over an electric heater with two 10-kW and four 5-kW independent elements. These are programmed, like the generators, to come on

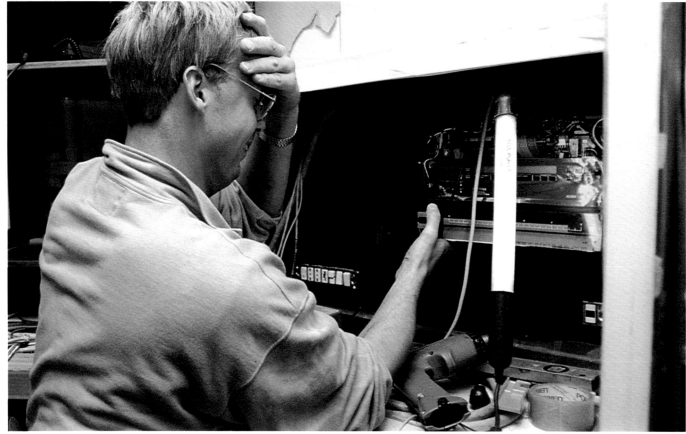

▲ *"Can all this electronics really fit into this small room?"*

▲ *Satellite dome on the down-to-earth mizzen mast.*

or off line in combinations just caloric enough to meet heating needs of the moment, with no excess consumption. Similarly, in warm weather the air is cooled and dried by air-conditioning units from Condaria, the Milan-based specialists who supply many shipyards with middle-capacity yacht cooling systems. The Condaria network serves up chilled air from four compressors, whose total cooling capacity of 192,000 BTU per hour is well in excess of what will be needed below, even in the sweltering tropics. With that redundancy, the units alternate, running in a sequence designed to equalize their usage over time and prolong their lives. And because they are also modular, one compressor can be popped out for repair or replacement without loss of total cooling. Each cabin has a hidden thermostat and fancoil, but temperature sensors are out in the rooms where they are more responsive. In a small galley cellar there is a separate cooler to keep vegetables and fruits fresh and crisp and hold a special bottle of *Pouilly-Fumé* ready if someone hooks a big, sweet bonito. (As the Polish proverb says: Fish, to taste right, must swim three times – in water, in butter and in wine.)

• ● •

Butter and wine may be basic to cooking, but water is the prime life-sustaining consumable on an oceangoing boat; it must be replenished regularly. The crew could set a catchment in the rain, but there are more consistent ways: When in harbor they can take fresh water into the circulating system from a hydrant, or fill the two 5,500-liter storage tanks; at sea they can allow tanks to be continually filled with sweet water by a high-capacity watermaker. No matter what the source, however, purity, sweetness and healthful quality are essential, so all fresh water passes through filters and an ultraviolet sterilizing unit, and the circulating system is configured to prevent stagnation and bacteria growth (salmonella grow well in untreated still water). The water is also subject to carbon filtration to sweeten the taste and eliminate odors.

The watermaker (actually it is a reverse-osmosis desalinator) is an SRC 15M3, made by Sea Recovery and installed by its Belgian distributor, Franken BV. Sea Recovery, in Gardena, California, has made watermakers for oil rigs, island resorts, remote camps, medical applications and luxury yachts since 1981, when it began pioneering the use of desalinators on fishing vessels (isn't it amazing how often fishermen get the good stuff first?). The 15M3 is capable of desalinating and purifying seawater at a healthy rate of 15,000 liters (4,000 US gallons) per day, operating continually. (Sea Recovery makes reverse-osmosis desalinators with capacities ranging between 750 and 95,000 liters per day.)

In *natural* osmosis, dissolved salts and minerals pass through a semipermeable membrane to equalize solutions on both sides. *Reverse* osmosis is an ingenious process in which salty, even contaminated seawater is forced through a membrane that *holds back* salts, minerals, spores, bacteria, viruses and algae, allowing only pure water to pass. While dissolved oxygen gives the water a reasonably natural taste, an odd but normal side effect of the process is its output of water that is slightly acidic. So to protect

▲ *Yes, all that electronics does fit in this small room!*

▲ *Starboard guest head, one of six to justify that watermaker.*

piping, delicate stomachs and the flavor of the morning coffee, the desalinated water passes through a limestone filter that dissolves enough calcium to neutralize it.

Juliet's water is circulated via a pressure tank that keeps the supply available without pumps running constantly. For hot water a boiler supplies the crew mess, a clothes washer in the forepeak and the galley (with its amazing three-minute, soapless dishwasher); a second boiler supplies the aft ship, with a booster to assure hot water for the owner's bath tub when the main supply drops below 40° C. The six Waterflash toilets also run on fresh water, using only about three liters per flush. And in case of rough weather, someone can push a button and drain all the toilets to prevent them from overflowing.

It is obvious that the single common element to all this fluid-transport is the common, humble pump. *Juliet* in fact has thirty-five pumps that move every sort of fluid – from sweet water to foul sludge to engine oil and fuel. Each is selected for its ability to best handle the viscosity, consistency, chemical and lubricating character of a particular fluid, and to meet the flow-rate, pressure and priming demands of the system it serves – which is why pumps are of piston, rotary, impeller, diaphragm or centrifugal type, and are made of steel, bronze, plastic, ceramic or rubber. Ten of those pumps come from one major supplier, Speck Pumps. Speck is an old family-run German company dating back to 1909, when a machinist named Daniel Speck and his eldest son Otto set up shop in Hilpolstein, near the great medieval city of Nuremberg,

birthplace of Albrecht Dürer. The company was re-formed in 1954 in Gartenberg, south of Munich, from a group of independent divisions that still operate in various German towns, each manufacturing its own line of highly specialized pumps, some of which are designed for such diverse usage as space suits, counter-swimming jets and boilers. For *Juliet*'s remarkable pump inventory, Speck's Dutch branch, in Zevenaar, supplied these special items: a self-priming piston pump for fridge and freezer sea water; two piston pumps to lift fresh water from the main tanks and one to fill the 110-liter pressure tank; a high-pressure deckwash pump; a high-output, high-speed portable firefighting pump; a slow-turning impeller sludge-removal pump; a large bilge manifold pump; a 3000-RPM centrifugal fuel-lift pump for the day tank, and a small sea-water circulating pump to keep lobsters alive in their very own deck box. Lowly, common pumps?

Sam Bos, Huisman's systems manager, was a key player in choosing those pumps and designing the pneumatics, hydraulics and refrigeration. Sam is a down-to-earth technician who likes to have his hands on the machinery he designs. He looks upon his work with a certain satisfied awe. "Sometimes the systems are too complex," he says. "We work all the time on them. We have a team, we sit around with drawings and we talk. We talk a lot. It is in our own interest to do the systems well, even if the owner doesn't understand them. But, *Juliet*'s owner has the knowledge. He makes you think. When it goes in harmony, it is good." For Sam, a little harmony goes a long way; but a pump or two won't hurt.

▲ *With a 15,000-liter desalinator, washdown is not wasteful.*

Should you need reminding at this juncture, *Juliet* is a *sailing* yacht. In addition to her engines, generators, worldwide communications and sophisticated plumbing, she has a tall, white and handsome rig and great white sails that, whenever the breeze blows fair and fresh, propel her with grace, rectitude and astonishing speed – Ron Holland and his client would have it no other way. But to attain that speed Holland had to first develop her sailplan. There was never any doubt that the client wanted her foresails to be the convenient roller-type, to which Holland agreed: Both the yankee and staysail are bent on to the largest Hydrofurls Rondal makes, model 300 HA. But as to the rest of the plan, the debate was vigorous. The client also inclined toward the convenience of roller-furling main and mizzen as well, but Holland, fresh from spectacular sailing results with *Cyclos III*, pressed for full-batten sails, whose added area would translate into greater speed, particularly on a reach. "We went back a forth a lot on this question," Holland recalls. "At one point we even considered a compromise boom-furling system with battens. But the client chose mast furling. It's hard to argue with pushbutton sailing, but if I had to do it again I

would still fight for a full-batten main." With that decision, the stage was set for Rondal's engineers to design the appropriate spars.

From 1975, when Wolter Huisman started Rondal, his spar and sailing-gear company, its specialists fabricated masts up to 45 meters from welded sections of aluminum extrusion bought from outside sources. In the late 1980s, using new data from mast-compression and rig-loading tests made aboard the Huisman-built 63-foot sloop *Yonder*, and finite-element analysis provided by Prof. Gerritsma at Delft University, Rondal's designers developed a better method of assembling longer masts from half-oval sections of plate that they could bend in-house, giving them greater freedom to design custom sections. The advantage of this type of mast is that it can be easily fabricated to taper continuously from heel to truck, making it light, flexible and aesthetically appealing. Rondal built such tapered masts for *Endeavour* and *Cyclos III*, and from those two yachts gathered more rig-load data for future standard masts.

But a furling mast is different animal: its sail-stowing chamber, greater girth and weight make its engineering more vexing. After tests of several methods, Rondal's designers elected to

▲ *The vast foredeck ... from an uncommon vantage point.*

three-quarter-oval shell forming the front and sides of the mast; a lateral reinforcing plate welded inside it; an internal half-circle furling-chamber opening aft, glued and screwed to the reinforcer; and a "U" shaped shell welded on to complete the back of the mast and enclose the furling chamber.

To achieve a continuous heel-to-truck taper (and 50 cm of calculated pre-bend) the six-meter lengths of shell plate were each cut and bent with a slight taper, the upper cross-section of each plate matching the bottom of the next higher plate. In assembling the mast, Rondal alternated the plates, like staggered brickwork, to spread the butt welds and avoid stress concentration and, as in the hull welding, they controlled heat distortion to prevent the mast from bending too much or in the wrong plane. A stainless-steel pipe for the mast washdown was inserted and when the mast was closed, the mainsail feeder slot was precision-cut by a laser-guided cutter and its edges were covered with a rounded anti-chafe channel. Spreader bases, light fittings and masthead platform were welded on, then the spar was ground smooth, chemically cleaned, faired and spray-painted and the furling rod, swivels, wiring conduit for lights, antennas, instruments, security camera and crow's nest controls were installed. With its spreaders (but no rigging) the mainmast weighs about 5,600 kilos. Even with computer aid, the design needed about 600 drawings and a good deal of sweat. The mizzen mast, on the other hand, was a relative snap: Just 33 meters long, equal to the mainmast of a mere 80-footer, it was built with only the top ten meters tapered.

Both masts are supported by high-tensioned shrouds and stays made by Riggarna Rigging Systems, based in England, with subsidiaries in the US, Sweden and France. Riggarna is a young, aggressive and small company that, from its inception in 1985, has supplied a steady stream of quality standing rigging to racing yachts, including maxis, level-raters, Whitbread entries and more than 30 America's Cup yachts in the 1991/92 campaign alone. In the late 1980s Riggarna entered the cruising yacht market, and in its first few years rigged some 40 yachts over 30 meters, including

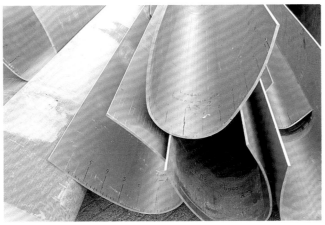

▲ *The first step toward a Rondal mast....*

▲ *The final step....*

a pair of 47-meter Perini Navi ketches and *Cyclos III*. The rigging Riggarna supplies, however, is not your everyday 1x19 wire; it is top-grade nickel/chromium/molybdenum-steel extruded rod, precisely dimensioned to handle the high static loads of a large rig without stretching, and to withstand the incredible shock loads induced by gusty winds, pitching and the frightful slamming of a hull into an unyielding sea. The quandary of designing a large sailboat rig, however, is that the support system has a narrow base less than the hull's maximum beam, which amplifies its loading, yet the rods cannot be made arbitrarily oversize for safety's sake, as the added weight and windage impair stability and sailing perform-ance. The rig's strength then comes from the rods' arrangement into truss-like supports based on the triangle (which John Roebling, creator of the Brooklyn Bridge, said was "the most indeformable geometric figure"). The mainmast's twenty triangles are formed by four pairs of spreaders in compression, eight vertical and twelve diagonal rods in tension (the lowest rod, called the V1, is just long enough to fit inside a 40-foot container, a consideration in the rig design). And where rods and spreader meet, they are joined by specialized Riggarna hardware with arcane names such as *tip cups* and *stemballs*, which by any other name would still serve to reduce rod wear, allow rod movement and subdue the arch-enemy of rod rigging: fatigue stress.

The base of the mainmast, trimmed to produce a 1.5-degree rake, sits on a massive aluminum shoe beneath the crew mess (where it is engulfed by an Art Deco stainless-steel handrail). The top of the mast, reached by bosun's chair or, for the faint-hearted, binoculars, is 159.6 feet (48.668 meters) over the water (33 feet short of Pisa's leaning tower but able to clear New York's Verrazano-Narrows Bridge by 57 feet at mean high water). From the masthead the view is on such an astral plane that even the most hardened bosun will be convinced he can see the Earth's curvature at the horizon. The mizzen, whose base is buried within the mahog-any of the aft quarters, has 0.5-degree rake and, with its bulbous SatCom dome, gives a more prosaic impression. Altogether, the

masts, shrouds, stays, jumpers and runners produce the structural tenacity and dynamic flexibility of a great suspension bridge; but they retain the felicitous proportion and subtle grace of a Greek column, in harmony with the hull – even when all sail is set.

• ● •

Robbie Doyle, who has always loved and been intrigued by sailing, stitched his first sail at the age of 14. It appeared to be only a casual event, however, as he later studied physics and planned a career in medicine. But in the early 1970s he was briefly side-tracked with a "temporary" job at Ted Hood's sail loft in Marblehead, Mass. In 1975 he took over the loft. In seven more years he set up his own. During that period he made lots of sails for production and custom racing and cruising boats, including those for the maxis *Equity in Law*, *Kialoa* and *Windward Passage*. But, as the racing world became more restrictive, in the late 1980s Doyle wisely shifted some of his efforts to the big-boat cruising market, producing suits of furling sails for boats such as *Freedom* (124') and *Andromeda* (145').

Out of his technical training and sailing skill (he was a successful racer himself, and involved with Ted Turner's America's Cup campaigns) Doyle developed a scientific approach to making sails: He uses computer programs to design them, lasers to cut them. He is also a philosopher, questioning how his work fits into the larger pattern of sport and life, which gives him a thoughtful historic approach to his work as well:

Decades ago, Doyle observes, every big-boat sail was made for a narrow wind range; yachts carried immense inventories and colossal crews, and incessant sail changes were the daily norm. Today, big boats have very small crews and owners want no soaking sailbags plopped on their damask upholstery; each sail now must work full time, without backup, hold its shape in a gale, draw well in a zephyr and withstand incessant rolling, reefing, flogging, deluging with seawater and searing by the sun. And it must be – by stubborn, universal client demand – white as the driven snow!

▲ *Fabrication and fairing: keys to a fine Rondal mast.*

▲ *The mizzen plays host to the photographer's daughter.*

▲ *Sail shaping, the old-fashioned way.*

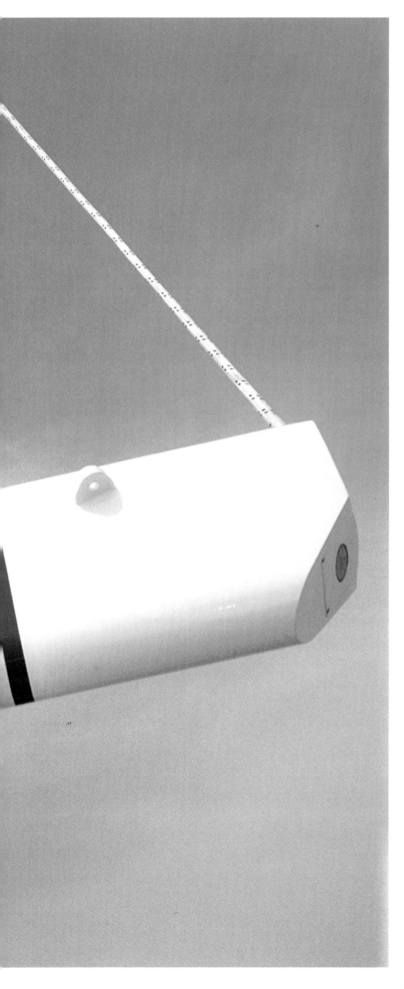

Juliet's Doyle sails are indeed white. But they didn't come by their color, or their form so easily. An ideal sail, to retain its shape as an airplane wing, should be made of a fabric that is light, everlasting and super-strong in all directions. No fabric offers all that, but some come close: Spectra is fine in tension, compression and flexure, but it "creeps" over time; Kevlar is stronger and less stretchy, but doesn't take bending or compression well; Dacron is durable and ultraviolet-resistent but it is too heavy for its strength. A judicious sandwich of all three, as Doyle serves up in his big sails, benefits from each fabric's best characteristics and still produces a sail half the weight and two to three times the strength of the best standard two-ply Dacron sail. (And, yes, by the marvel of chemistry, it is white.)

But cloth alone does not guarantee a good roller-furling sail. The furling sail is notoriously harder to cut than a non-furling one: it tends to have poor airfoil shape, it is too full and its leech hooks to windward, increasing drag. And once set, its loose foot and lack of battens make it difficult to flatten properly on the wind or for reaching in a breeze. If the sail's panels are cut, however, to align the fabric strength with the load pattern (as calculated by computer for upwind conditions), the sail holds a flatter shape when close hauled, but is still readily rounded out for sailing off the wind. Thus Doyle cut *Juliet*'s mainsail with panels that form catenaries – natural load-distributing curves like bridge cables – that concentrate fabric strength toward the sail's center of effort. Foam-filled spring-metal battens support the leech, keeping it from curling, but wrap neatly when the sail is furled.

The yankee and staysail, which are not bent on to rigid spars (they are bent onto flexible stays and furlers) have different load concentrations. They take the greater stress in their leech and foot, where their catenary panels help retain shape in a strong breeze. In that breeze, *Juliet*'s yankee clew may endure as much as 10 metric tons of pull. That sort of high tension has been known to melt a bowline from internal friction, or excite a natural resonance that turns the clew ring into a "sabre saw" than can buzz right through heavily reinforced fabric. And when the sail flogs, as during a tack, the heavy clew shackles menace painted masts and rod rigging (which can weaken at the slightest nick or dent).

Considering all this, Doyle designed a "soft" clew with radially arranged webbing eyes joined to the sheet by a light, continuous lacing. The lacing spreads the load over a wide clew area and absorbs shock, and the sheet-end needs only a thimble for the lacing (no melting bowline, no cutting buzz saw, no menacing shackle). And it's all leather-encased for padding, chafe resistance and good looks.

In designing the sails to the required precision, Doyle had to coordinate with Ron Holland and Rondal early on, to avoid mis-

▲ *Staysail dousing, the modern way.*

fitting sails. Righting moments were considered, as *Juliet*'s greater stability than similar boats adds to her rig loads. Factors such as mast pre-bend, sheeting angles and headstay tensions also played integral roles in crafting optimum panels that hold their shape while all else is bending around them (even minuscule hull flexing affects tensions). As Doyle says: "Sail design is not dart throwing; it is science." In Doyle's hands, it is also art.

• • •

But how can just six sailors (including a 110-pound cook) prevail over 887 square meters of white working sails, 700 square meters of white reaching sails (mizzen staysail and MPS) and 3,000 linear meters of colorful running rigging? In the preliminary design, Ron Holland and Rob Jacob drew a deck arrangement for just that purpose, setting sheeting angles, fairleads, winches and turning blocks. But it changed progressively under many influences, technical and cosmetic. Holland felt, for example, that *Juliet*, like *Cyclos*, could be sailed comfortably with large hydraulic drum winches. Wolter Huisman agreed. But the client wanted the new style of captive reel winches, and the client, as before and after, got his way. But, where to put them? Mounting the large primary winches under the deck near the mast was considered, but that would have devoured interior volume and created tormented sheeting paths. So the designers placed the winches – main, yankee and staysail sheets, traveler and runners – at deck level, inside the port and starboard cockpit coamings, which devoured only some pilothouse area, a small price to pay.

And what of the winches themselves? Wolter Huisman is a conservative thinker; for years he had resisted installing existing reel winches because of problems he observed: When winding on under heavy load the sheet may override itself, disabling the winch; when winding off, kinks may develop that jam at the outlet; rotational speeds (power settings) are limited to a few choices; mechanisms suffer from salt, grime and poor maintenance. The only way Wolter would satisfy the client and himself was to design a new reel winch, from scratch. So the Rondal RW 8000 (the large economy size) was born. To avoid overrides, the sheet is fed by a worm-geared fairlead onto a reel large enough to accept the full sheet in

▲ *The Doyle clew gets a close inspection.*

▲ *Fabricating the prototype Rondal captive reel winch.*

▲ *Despite hydraulics, you still have to read the "woolies."*

one layer (35 meters for *Juliet's* yankee alone); to avoid kinks, the unwinding sheet is pulled out of the coaming by a small winch at the outlet so it never goes slack; to provide versatile power and speed, the winches (except mizzen sheet and mizzen outhaul) are proportionally controlled; and to minimize maintenance headaches the gearing is sealed in oil (Rondal recommends an oil change just once every ten years).

The runner winches are also Rondal RW 8000s, but the runners have a separate foreguy. Runners are dangerous; when released they can thrash into the rigging or injure crew. So the foreguys, secured to the upper runner blocks, are under constant tension, pulled by small reel winches under the deck; as a runner is slacked during a maneuver it is hauled, still under tension itself, to the shrouds without attention from the crew. The runners also have unique Rondal deck blocks – consisting of a housing with stainless-steel rollers arrayed in an arc that equals the turning angle – half the size of a single, needlessly large sheave. Blocks of this design are used on the main and mizzen outhaul slides as well, and the two-part mainsheet has half-blocks that permit extremely close sheeting of the boom to its massive arch.

Oddly, after insisting on hiding the primary winches, the owner – who had once found *Aquel II* "too winchless" – asked for a few drums on deck just "to make *Juliet* look like a sailboat." There are more practical reasons, though, why she has two Rondal eight-ton hydraulic drum winches and two smaller Lewmars at the mast. They are used, among other purposes, to raise halyards. But halyard loads are taken by Rondal snubbing winches and cleats under the deck, which leaves the power winches free for other work such as overhauling mooring lines. Two big Rondal hydraulic winches aft, near the mizzen mast, handle mooring lines astern.

Those mooring lines and all other working line aboard *Juliet* – sheets, halyards, lower runners and utility lines – were stranded and braided in a variety of bright, coded colors, in suitable diameters and of appropriate strengths by the Bremen-based German company Geo. Gleistein & Sohn GmbH. Gleistein, one of the world's leading purveyors of running rigging, began making marine ropes way back in the 1820s, a period in maritime

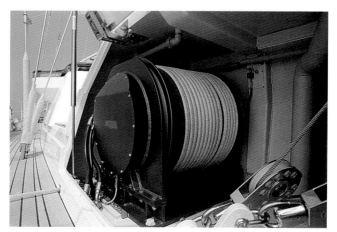

▲ *Starboard runner reel winch.*

history when the only cordage fibers available were those gleaned from nature's bounteous trees and plants – sisal (*agave*), manila (*abaca*) and hemp (*cannabis*). Gleistein still uses large quantities of these rough and strong natural fibers to satisfy the undiminished hunger for traditional rope aboard cargo and passenger ships and working vessels. But today Gleistein specializes in spinning and weaving a vast catalogue of yacht-quality line that is strong, flexible and soft to the hand, from chemically produced chain-molecule fibers with clinical names such as polypropylene, polyester, polyamid, polyethylene and aramid, which are marketed under popular names as Spectra, Kevlar, Dyneema and Twaron. *Juliet's* Gleistein sheets are combinations of these fibers, mostly with Kevlar cores and Spectra covers to assure the endurance and strength needed to withstand years of ten-ton loads and heavy chafing as they flog in the breeze and wind on and off the winches.

• • •

The exact placement of those winches and every other item of deck gear was the subject of many early planning meetings. A deck is not a detached sail-working platform, planned in isolation; like every other aspect of design its shaping and equipping impinge on other features. One great concern in a deck plan is its potential conflict with the interior, as when a winch is needed where a hatch is wanted. Jurrie Zandbergen, whose bailiwick includes deck design, feels strongly about this everyday conflict: "When you have to make a choice between a winch and a hatch, then there will be no hatch, or else you can't sail. Sailing always wins."

Zandbergen may have been feeling a bit optimistic at the moment he said that, as few people know better than he does that nothing in *Juliet's* long and difficult creation was ever that straight-forward. Consider this following brief survey of how some of the other major deck features were set in place, which to some may read more like the design treatise for a 100-clown circus Volkswagen than a megasailer's operating deck:

To begin with: How do you stow three inflatable dinghies and a luscious 12-foot clinker-built mahogany sailboat, using the minimum space, making them accessible and easy to launch, without scratching the brightwork? You first design a foredeck well for the largest inflatable; that's easy. But rather than stow the others casually under a ton of gear, you design a transom garage for them. But when the owner questions its structural integrity and the risk of getting back aboard in a lumpy sea, you turn the transom into a magnificent hydraulically opening swim platform and design a big lazarette with a 14-foot hatch on the afterdeck to stow the clinker dinghy (along with four touring bikes, a racing bike, several surf-boards, two outboards, two windsurfers, a gaggle of oars, life jackets, water skis, inflatable beach toys, swim ladders, fishing gear, golf clubs, spares, tools, oils, greases, varnishes, canvas

▲ *Stainless-steel fittings, all from Rondal's workshop.*

covers, the dive compressor with bottles and a "shore pack" (with a barbecue and who-knows-what-else). That leaves no room for the medium dinghy, which you decide must be lashed on deck, partly deflated, under the main boom.

To stow the clinker you snugly strap it to the underside of the 14-foot lazarette hatch, where it sits on a small cradle. If you leave it strapped to the hatch, when you open the hatch the clinker comes with it allowing access to the rack of toys and boards beneath it. But if you first unstrap the clinker, when you open the hatch the dinghy awaits launching from its cradle with a halyard. To make room for launching it, however, you are forced to split the mizzen backstay and move the pushpit-mounted antennas, leaving no room for a stern anchor. Then, to carry the third dinghy, you make 50 drawings just to design quite the most elaborate davits ever made: Their arms telescope; their cables self-adjust length as the arms telescope, and pressure-control flow valves equalize cable tensions to keep the dinghy level as it rides up or down. But that clever idea forces you to shift the stern light, stern passarelle, pushpit stanchions and corner seats. One bonus: the davits make a perfect platform on which to set the kayaks (but, in the interest of safety, only for short inshore runs).

The rest of *Juliet*'s deck is a domain of painstakingly placed custom fittings: 15 stainless-steel Rondal cowl vents (stamped out of one piece then polished to mirror quality); a dozen stainless Rondal cleats and bollards with custom mushroom-cap heads; ten glowing juice-squeezer prisms mounted flush at select points that inject and radiate natural light into the crew quarters; stainless-steel roller fairleads in the bulwarks for the twelve mooring lines and a magnificent Comar hydraulic side passarelle that stows under the starboard deck and deploys, at a button's push, by sliding out straight, then rotating aft as it pivots down and self-articulates its steps.

There is one final element of *Juliet*'s deck design and construction that must, like nearly all the rest, serve in silence, over many years and against all odds. It is subject to the vagaries of salt, sun and sand; it is ever being impinged upon by gritty shoes, calloused feet, flogging sails, whipping sheets, dropped anchors, sliding dinghies, dragged outboards and big pieces of hard airline luggage; and it is forever being marauded by pollutants, oils, chemicals, detergents, brushes, cleansers, fuels, lotions, drinks and the occasional gob of mayonnaise. It is *Juliet*'s stunning teak deck, assembled by joiners from some 1,500 separate parts, each flawlessly cut, aligned and bedded. If laid end-to-end those 1,500 teak strips would total about 4.5 kilometers (2.8 miles) – or some fifteen Eiffel Towers. And there it lies, without blemish, without complaint, looking so natural, as though no one had given so much as a thought to its design. Nonsense.

▲ *The craftsman's hand, the crown of teak decking.*

GETTING THE "RIGHT FEELING"

"Without plan there can be neither grandeur of aim and expression, nor rhythm, nor mass, nor coherence. . . ." – Le Corbusier

"Sleep faster. We need the pillows." – Yiddish Saying

A yacht interior is a womb, a personal domain of warmth and regeneration; as such, it may well be the most important aspect of any new custom yacht. Inviting a stranger to design an interior for you, therefore, is like lending your fountain pen – it rarely works well. As a result, many desperate clients commission their house architect, their spouse or their eccentric cousin with a degree in art history to do the design, just to avoid the stress of forging yet another new relationship in a program already over-stressed by too many new relationships. Though Pieter Beeld-snijder was not a total stranger when he entered the fray in 1988, he recalls that the innovative nature of the project still challenged him to forge a basically new partnership with the client.

"This was a giant project for a complicated man. He was searching for a new impressive style. He knew what he wanted deep inside; it just took a long time to come out. He loves corners – inviting corners with lots of cushions and good sightlines. He likes to sit and talk with friends, on deck or in the saloon, to eat below yet see outside. He likes long visual lines, moody lighting; he dislikes shocks, things overdone. He likes to hang out, in a couch or in a corner, to feel that it fits like an old T-shirt. He wants magazines and books everywhere so anyone can grab something to read, even in the bathtub. He likes to see the appliances in the galley, so it *feels* like a galley and is just a comfortable space to hang out. Every space on this boat is comfortable, every corner is its own universe, a place to hang out."

To create corners for hanging out you first need to draw a general arrangement – the allocation of space to sleeping, social and service areas. More than just a fixing of walls and openings, the general arrangement is, in the architect Louis Kahn's words, "a society of rooms." It reckons with traffic flow and views, air and light, communality and solitude and, on a yacht, the accursed engine room (it was Beeldsnijder who pushed the hardest for the in-line engine to gain saloon height without raising the house). In working out the arrangement, Beeldsnijder spent long hours with

▲ *Pieter Beeldsnijder: ever in thought, ever on the move.*

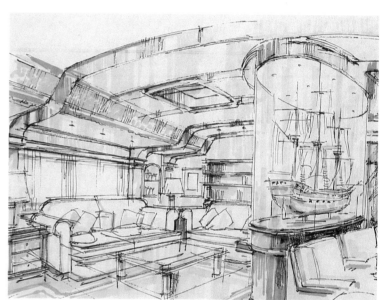

Some of Pieter Beeldsnijder's attempts to get "that feeling."

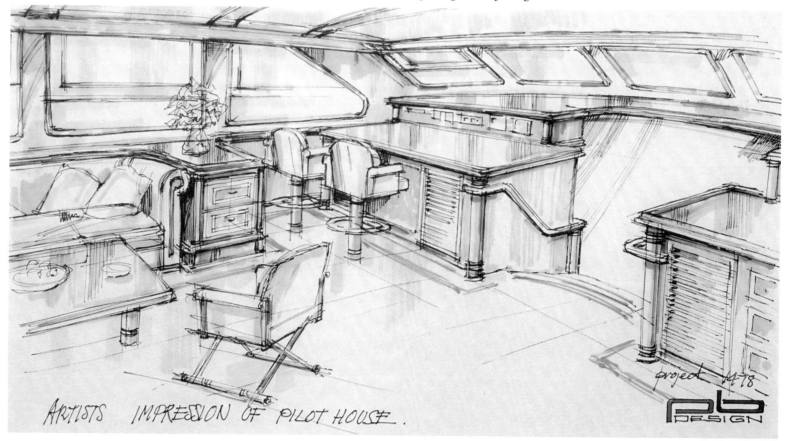

ARTISTS IMPRESSION OF PILOT HOUSE.

project 1478

pb DESIGN

▲ *Port-side in the deckhouse: its own universe …*

the client, as they tried to visualize walking around, sitting in each seat, relating to other people, even opening doors. After a year and dozens of plans of boats between 105 and 135 feet, in May 1989, with the owner's suite, two guest cabins, saloon, deckhouse and crew quarters in place, Beeldsnijder squeezed in the small spare cabin to port and the radio-navigation room to starboard and *Juliet*'s growth halted at 143 feet.

In the layout, Beeldsnijder consciously avoided symmetry and rigidity: Stairs and passageways are off centerline; floor levels vary to diversify sightlines, and twenty-two asymmetrically arranged hull ports and deckhouse windows create ever-changing views to the outside. And he formed those corners in every place possible. The deckhouse has two cozy corners: a settee to starboard and two to port, each with fine outside views. From the deckhouse, a spiral-bannistered stairway descends to the saloon, where a formal dining corner to starboard centers on a majestic oval table with firmly upholstered settees, and a snug social corner to port is formed by two overstuffed sofas. Between them stands a stunning antique model of a 17th-century ship, the *Anson*, set on an octagonal base containing nautical charts and the electric piano keyboard. Standing like a glass-enclosed oak tree, the ship model is both a fulcrum for and a partition between the austerity of the dining corner and the softness of the living corner. Sunlit by day, incandescent by night, it is a central beacon for any guest aboard, and it can be seen (by design) from the owner's suite, more than 50 feet aft.

That suite is the epitome of all that is admirable and lovely about *Juliet*'s interior design and finish – a gently lighted, softly cushioned, pale-colored realm ideal for rest, contemplation or work, cocooned in deep, roseate mahogany. Like everything else aboard, selecting the wood and its panel format came only after much searching by Beeldsnijder and the client – through books, magazines, galleries and even a hotel lobby or two. The client initially fussed over a host of natural wood veneers, one-by-one rejecting golden oak, sallow cherry, ultra-Scandinavian teak and exquisitely grained Australian lacewood (which he found in an airport lounge, but is too fragile for a yacht). The turning point came when the two men found shared inclination toward both Art

▲ *… and the larger universe of the saloon.*

Deco and "Biedermeier," an eclectic post-Napoleonic German composite of Greco-Roman Classicism, French Empire and English Regency styles, for which mahogany is an ideal base. Beeldsnijder's Biedermeier, however, embodies fresh details such as grains that play tricks with the eye and Greek-Revival columns that pop out for varnishing. And because it is for a yacht, his broadly curved corners, rounded edges and oversize fiddles promote safety for hands and bodies, as they invite caressing by the eye.

Juliet's woodwork, not easily designed, was less easily built. Willem Slingerland, the yard's youthful interior project manager, knows this well. "We are in a very high class of furniture making," he says. "The construction quality must be consistent throughout; that is why we always make our own veneers." A trained carpenter and draftsman, Slingerland took the client around to suppliers to help him select the particular Brazilian swietenia mahogany, ebony-like wenge inlays and madrona burls that engulf the guest accommodations. He made test pieces for the client to approve grain and color. He displayed fabrics, leathers, marbles and wood samples in a unique cabinet that subjects them to every sort of lighting – natural and artificial – to assess their compatibility. He detailed each cabin and scheduled construction drawings. In the summer of 1990, a year after *Juliet*'s size was fixed, those drawing were finally handed over to Adriaan Voerman.

Voerman is the Huisman chief joiner. Like woodworkers everywhere, he has a quiet demeanor, tough hands and an unpretentious concept of his art. He portrayed his joiners' formidable encounter with *Yard Project No.357* this way: "Pieter Beeldsnijder did drawings. We checked them to see that it would all fit. We returned the drawings for corrections. Then we purchased the wood, made the veneer and built the furniture." Conceding only that "mahogany is a difficult wood that comes in too many colors and grades to easily match," Voerman's supreme modesty masks two intense years of painstaking technical and sensual merging of a wide spectrum of wood to satisfy a demanding client.

Wood is a capricious product of nature – its fragrance and dust are the only elements common to all shipyards, no matter their primary building material – metal, composite or plastic. But,

▲ *The joinery shop …*

▲ ... where "fit and finish" take on profound meaning.

▲ *Forty joiners: seeking uniformity in wood …*

... creating diversity in wood.

though wood lacks the artificial uniformity of those manmade materials, clients often expect as much uniformity from shipyard joiners. Voerman and his team did somehow manage to match wood that grew on several continents and was processed by several companies. For example, the high-grade marine plywood he used for furniture structures came from Bruynzeel Multipanel, of Zaandam; the closed-cell PVC and paper-cell honeycomb sandwich panels he used as the base for furniture, bulkhead and door veneering came from Woodindustry Bros. van Rozendaal, of Schijndel; the solid mahogany for fiddles, moldings and joints and the teak for the crew quarters came from Van Hout, of Mill.

Van Hout is typical of large wood suppliers. It imports wood from Africa, Russia, America and South Asia, converting about 30,000 cubic meters (one million cubic feet) of logs per year into solid board, plywood and veneer. Most logs are 80 years old when they are cut down, and they are allowed to dry out for two years before conversion. Still, 50 percent of hardwood logs have knots or poor grain that disqualify them for fine furniture, and 95 percent are "too nervous" for making delicate veneer. (Veneer sheets are produced in two ways: by a "straight" method in which a rigidly held log slowly advances sideways into a surging guillotine, which shaves off paper-thin slices that are edge-glued into long sheets; or a "rotary" method in which the log spins between mandrels and slowly advances into a blade that peels off a continuous sheet. In either method a single log goes a long way.)

To build the furniture, Voerman's joiners glued sheets of veneer to appropriate panels and assembled each piece, adding inlays, surrounds and moldings according to the dozens of detailed drawings created by Jan Been and his small team of interior drafts-men. In the process, they rejected four cubic meters of already-purchased mahogany, approved by the supplier but not of adequate quality for Huisman's fine furniture. They also engineered the backs of the built-in furniture, according to drawings, shaping the structural wood to properly dovetail with the aluminum frame-work, pipes, wires and ducting already in place. Smaller pieces were built complete; larger ones that didn't fit through deck openings were built in sections and assembled inside. Joiners also

▲ *Installing the big furniture pieces …*

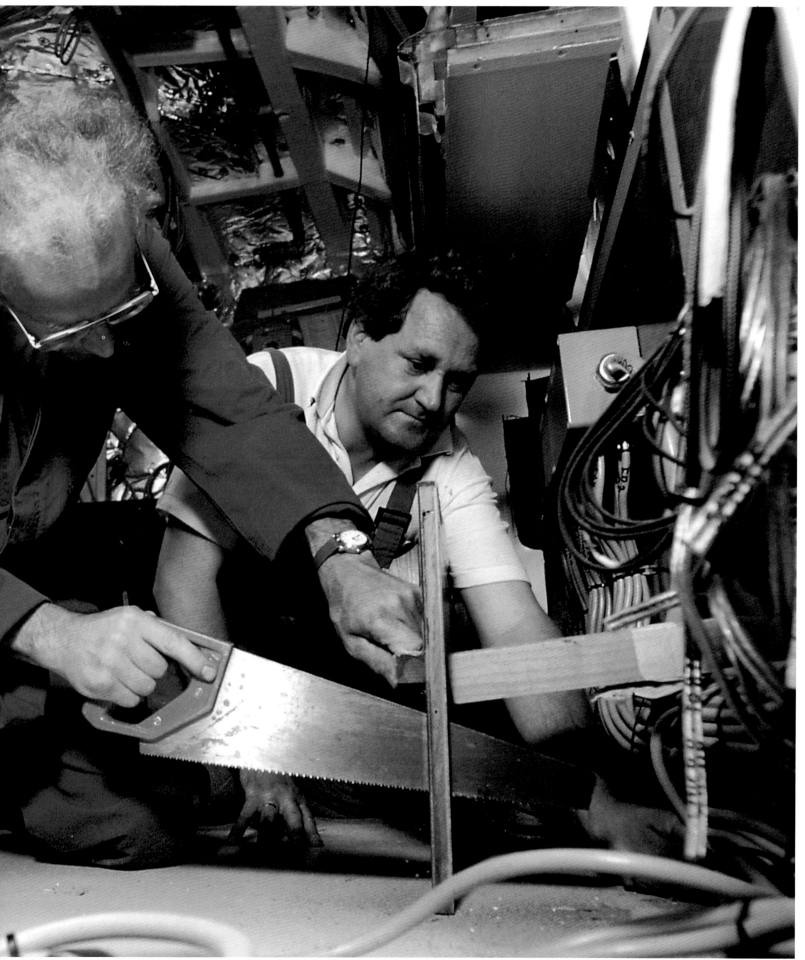

▲ … sometimes requires a bit of "engineering."

built the broad veneered bulkheads that separate cabins, boring long holes inside their foam coring so that when the client later chose locations for many outlets, switches or telephones (*after* the bulkheads were in place) electricians had the choice of channels through which to run the wiring. Nothing is easy.

Finally, to achieve the required depth of finish on all the mahogany woodwork, it was stained with an alcohol/water dye, sealed, brushed with a thin coat of polyurethane matte varnish, lightly sanded, brushed with two coats, sanded, sprayed with two coats, sanded, sprayed twice again, sanded, then given several finish coats. The teak in the crew quarters was also treated with paint and varnish supplied by Hasco, a Dutch producer of high quality interior/exterior finishes. This sustained process of construction and finishing explains clearly why nearly one-third of all the yard's workers are carpenters and joiners, and why Voerman refers softly but proudly to their end result as *vakman-schap* (which translates, so inadequately, into *craftsmanship*).

Meanwhile Slingerland's work continued. He helped find door handles, cabinet glass, mirrors, carpeting, marble and bathroom fixtures. From Almere, Holland, he selected crew cabin upholstery, sheets, duvets, and the Novasuede overhead liner from Hendriks Interiors. He assigned the making of the octagonal vitrine for the ship model to the Emmeloordse Glashandel, of Emmeloord, Holland. And he bought socket outlets, cover plates and light switches by the hundreds. As Pieter Beeldsnijder so often says, "the effort is in the details," and such a small detail as a well-designed light switch can make a large impact on the livability and looks of a yacht. The switches chosen for *Juliet*, therefore, do more than just turn lights on and off; they are clever, responsive, and very Italian – made by BTicino, a world-class environmental-electrics design house in high-fashion, high-tech Milan.

From its seeding in the 1950s as an industrial design firm, BTicino germinated into a major manufacturer of intelligent, stylish household and industrial products. It now is fully committed to a practice it likes to call "Electrical Architecture," a conscious synergy with industrial designers, commercial and house architects to create beautifully designed electrical contrivances with multiple

▲ *The owner's marble bathroom.*

▲ *The owner's mahogany-encased office suite.*

functions. (Wise mariners know that any item on a boat that has just one function should be deep-sixed immediately.) In BTicino's hands, no longer does the lowly light switch have just one function; it is now part of a larger system – call it a habitat. So, for example, most of *Juliet*'s 160 BTicino light switches are set in panels that control at least two sets of lights in their assigned space. A guest can touch one or two buttons and set spots, picture lights and strips, bringing them on dimmed or fully lighted in combinations to suit (or create) a mood. And the lighting of the saloon, with its 1,569 individual light sources, has its own dedicated BTicino "mood control" center tucked in a small panel in the mahogany side board on the stairway, whose buttons can blend all manner of light levels, from a halogen shout to a candle-dim incandescent whisper. Even the cover plates are dedicated to style: in the fore-ship, they are flat brass as befits the white-painted wood and teak trim; aft, they are custom formed to imitate in miniature the Beeldsnijder panelling. And, yes, they do turn lights off as well.

Acting as another person's inner eye can be an enormous burden; Pieter Beeldsnijder thinks he used 3,000 meters of paper in designing the interior. "I had to live with the finished work for a year or two before even I realized just how everything works," he recalls. "I had to grow into it." That is how complicated a yacht can get. The photographs on these pages, therefore, can only reveal the facade, the matte-varnished skin, of *Juliet*'s brilliantly conceived, decorously built, lovingly finished interior. As a result, though the camera tells a glowing story, the camera also leaves much unre-vealed. The photos also seem to record an elegance too exalted for "hanging out," another instance of the disingenuous, the uncandid, camera. *Juliet*, despite the magnificence of her surface finish, is truly a womb, a place for warmth and regeneration, a place for hanging out. She and her owner invite guests to remove their shoes, sit on her floors, sink into her sofas and curl up in her corners. Beeldsnijder says: "My job was to get a nice feeling all around." Slingerland says: "My job was to work with the client and architect to get that feeling as nice as possible." But it took 40 Huisman joiners two years of long workdays to turn that feeling into real, solid but lightweight furniture.

▲ *Silver dinner service for twenty-four …*

▲ *… and an elegant snack for the crew.*

LAUNCHED!

"The achieve of, the mastery of the thing!" – G. M. Hopkins

On April 3, 1993 – one thousand eight hundred forty-one days after the client arrived in Vollenhove to "buy a boat and go sailing" – that boat's interior was about finished, her exterior painting was done, and she was ready to leave. No, she was not ready to *sail away*; six weeks more of intensive, sometimes frantic, work lay ahead of her. It was simply time for her to leave the paint shed, where she had been in residence for two months; time, in fact, to leave the shipyard and Vollenhove altogether, so that her worthy successor *Borkumriff*, a classic 40-meter Lunstroo schooner, might deservedly move up a notch in the construction sequence, followed by *Saudade*, a modern 33-meter Judel & Vrolijk sloop and two 20.5-meter Henry Scheel jewels.

Moving a Huisman yacht is always a big local event, even on a Saturday. A few workers gathered and townsfolk gawked from across the canal and along the road. Only horses grazing nearby treated it as an ordinary gray spring day. But it assuredly was not. You see, though Wolter moved the shipyard to Vollenhove in 1971 to find deeper water, his largest yachts have become too deep-keeled for him to launch into the canal there; and even if he could launch them, the IJsselmeer, with as little as three meters of water, isn't deep enough to sail them away. Like *Endeavour* and *Cyclos* before her, to be launched *Juliet* would have to be shipped 55 nautical miles over the IJsselmeer, to Harlingen. On a barge.

And what a bizarre process this barging is! Weighing in at about 215 metric tons (with no rig, no fuel, no water or golf clubs aboard yet) *Juliet* had to first be set on a unique hydraulic 12-axle flatbed brought in by Lommerts, the Dutch transportation special-ists. Lommerts – whose cranes and trucks have carried power plant generators, prefabricated bridges and windmills (old and new) from one end of Europe to the other – are wizards at moving cumbersome loads over long distances. This time the load was no

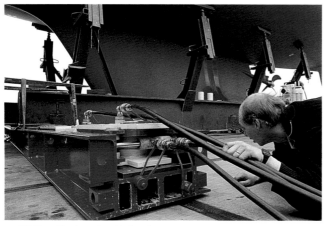

▲ *Sliding the beast onto her barge.*

▲ *The angler eyes a big one.*

▲ *The second bridge, gateway to the IJsselmeer.*

▲ Juliet*'s first ride on the open, freshwater sea …*

less cumbersome but the distance was just 200 meters. The team jacked her onto the flatbed and rolled her slowly around the shed and parked her at the quayside where a new custom-built 63-meter steel barge awaited. She was gently slid by hydraulic rams onto the barge, and on Wednesday morning workers inched the cradle further to the side, until it sat precariously on the barge's starboard edge, while they water-ballasted the port side to maintain trim. Two tugs arrived, tied up fore and aft and hauled the barge carrying *Juliet* and three containers filled with her gear, spares and the shipyard's two portable workshops out into the narrow canal.

But, as it is everywhere in Holland, just 300 meters ahead lies a typical Dutch roadway bridge, of such dimensions that even when it is swung fully up it is impossible for something so large as *Juliet* to pass through. The Dutch, however, are masters of the impossible. That is why she was set on the barge off-center: so as she traversed the bridge opening her starboard bilge would ride just *over* the roadway edge while her port rail would slip just *under* the tilted bridge span. To accomplish this the water level in the canal had to be within a critical three-centimeter range. With the wind's cooperation, it was, and the barge literally scraped through the gap as workers on deck held thin carpeted pads to fend off the varnish. Watching from the other side of the bridge the owner said it suggested the birth of "an impossibly large baby." Indeed, passing through that bridge, *Juliet* did emerge from her "birth canal," and without a scratch.

Back on centerline, *Juliet* and her escort passed through another, narrow bridge, then the tugmen added pontoons alongside for stability and the barge and its precious newborn cargo were hauled slowly northward along the IJsselmeer's eastern shore. Thursday morning the odd trio entered the imposing locks at Kornwerderzand, at the eastern terminus of the Afsluitdijk, the prodigious 30-kilometer dam that keeps Holland from being swallowed by the North Sea, and they were lifted three meters from fresh water to salt. When the locks opened, they trundled the last few nautical miles to the cavernous drydock facility of the Frisian Shipyard in Harlingen, completing an almost irreversible voyage:

▲ *... and her introduction to the salty sea.*

▲ *The owner's beaming mother launches her son's dream.*

Because of this absolutely aggravated process *Juliet*, like *Cyclos* and *Endeavour*, may someday return, but not on her own bottom.

On Friday, April 9, 1993, in a grim city-size ship-building shed, dimmed by a gray wind-driven mist but brightened by pre-arranged yellow tulips, purple irises and silver buckets of chilling champagne, the owner, his parents, friends, the crew, the Huisman team and family, Pieter Beeldsnijder and his wife Willy, two TV crews, Robbie Doyle and Wubbo Ockels (a Dutch astronaut) gathered to share the long-awaited moment of *Juliet*'s launch. But like her caesarian-style birth, her delivery to the water did not go easily either. After some hours of preparation, she was held in slings by a double 100-ton overhead crane forward and a mobile 400-tonner aft. At about 1400, on signal from a shipyard director, their cables simultaneously tensed, strained and finally hummed as they lifted her as high as they might to clear the cradle. But there was a snag: The containers on the barge were too tall to clear the keel and rudder, and the tug was unable to pull the barge out from under. She was suspended perilously in time and space until mechanics could make hydraulic adjustments to allow the big crane to lift higher. The barge was finally slipped out and at 1700 *Juliet* was lowered until her keel nearly touched the water.

At this precipitous point the owner's mother – a petite, vibrant sweetheart – gave a brief speech with love-filled words about her son's great dream, praise for the workers who helped him realize it and blessings for *Juliet*'s safe voyaging. Then she swung the champagne bottle, concluding: "I christen thee *Juliet*." Bang! The bottle burst, the cranes lowered the hull slowly into the water and hugs, kisses, cheers and more champagne followed. Jurrie Zandbergen, who had done the final weight calculations, pointed with certainty (and relief?) to her precise flotation; Jan Bokxem (whom the owner had said "reached burnout months before") smiled genuinely; Wolter beamed like a grandfather (which he is, several times), and everybody toasted and went off to a big Australian-style barbecue as only the Dutch can rustle up.

But after dinner there was more work, as a total of 80 meters and 15,000 kilos of fully rigged main and mizzen masts,

▲ *Essential launch ingredients.*

▲ *Crown Prince Willem Alexander "takes the conn."*

which had come up earlier by barge, had to be stepped by Rondal's chief rigger, Herman Slot, conducting an orchestra whose instruments were a giant forklift, a towering crane and twenty men wielding guylines (and a lot of cool savvy when a strong breeze suddenly sprung up). Someone remembered at the last moment to drop a coin, a US dime, under the mainmast as it slipped onto its shoe (an essential ritual of good fortune). By nightfall, in the glare of orange mercury-vapor lamps and against a fading western sky, the riggers pinned the shrouds and stays, the Rondal rig stood tall and firm and there, before the crowd's moistened eyes, *Juliet* was transformed from a bare hull into a balanced ketch.

But far from ready to sail. Over the next two weeks a score of Huisman workers – some arriving daily, some living with a dog, a parrot and a private chef on a hired hotel barge named *Vita Pugna* (The Fighting Life?) – continued to fine-tune her inside and out. From early morning to late evening they shuffled between the portable workshops and the boat to finish wiring, lighting, woodwork and rigging. Suppliers trucked in material and gear, while subcontractors with briefbags full of technical manuals came to tune their products. Huisman workers, in blue coveralls, crawled into cabinetry, bilges and overheads, and poked around the engine room, joined by visitors in red, yellow, green or white coveralls who consulted, advised and consented. Watching this technical rainbow coalition solving a hundred riddles reminded a visitor of an observation made by the astute, accomplished project manager Jan Bokxem, many months earlier: "We cannot build a boat alone," he said. "We don't know everything. We depend on our suppliers for much information and much help." Such is the making of a great yacht – by a shipyard that knows its limitations.

On select days, under Wolter's watchful eye, *Juliet* was taken out for systems and machinery trials in the hands of Michael Koppstein. Koppstein is the former captain of *Whirlwind XII* and the Huisman yard's US representative. Because the yard is responsible for a yacht until she is transferred to her owner, Koppstein takes command of sea trials. His functions are to demonstrate to the owner and permanent crew that the yacht meets contract speci-

▲ *Through a bridge, lightly, under her own power.*

Juliet

▲ *Beeldsnijder, a friend and the scintillating North Sea.*

fications, to share his operating experience with the crew and give them an opportunity to stand back and observe without feeling pressure to make decisions. *Juliet*'s trials, performed according to protocols designed by Erik van Hulst (the bright, poised and young Huisman manager in charge of performance assurance and warranty), tested steering, propulsion, gearbox, autopilot and thrusters under real-life conditions for the first time. But these tests were almost perfunctory: Wolter, knowing well in advance that *Juliet* would be late in coming together, and foreseeing the risks of last-minute sea-trial hitches, had instructed the systems engineers to perform many tests during the summer of 1992, while *Juliet* was still under construction. They had set a pump at the canal's edge and supplied water to the construction shed for engine, generators, air-conditioners, desalinator and thrusters; thus they had fired up most of the important heavy machinery, at least under partial load, allowing for easier sea trials later.

On Saturday, 24 April, as planned, *Juliet* took a pilot aboard and headed out of Harlingen, past the islands of Terschelling and Vlieland, and turned southwest to Den Helder, where there is more open water suitable for lengthy sailing trials. One observant guest made these notes during the brief "offshore" passage:

"Beautiful weather: 12-15 knots southwest. Passed an armada of traditional boats setting sail. All action stopped; they were stunned by us. The engine was tested at various pre-specified loads. Two guys from MTU [in coveralls, of course] climbed all over the engine with thermometers and stethoscopes. The trial was absolutely uneventful – one would think it was the 755th in a long series, not the first. Pampered by nice food: Pea soup for lunch. After lunch, Wolter said: *Well, boys, let's see some sails!* Winches hummed. No one shouted. Boat heeled and paced off on North Sea at 14 knots. One of owner's wide-eyed friends said: *She sails like a 250-ton Ferrari*."

But the same observant guest also made note of the unexpected: "Owner never insisted on taking wheel. Never got in anyone's way. Stayed below. Listened to a variety of music. Behaved as a child when he discovered sea swirling by the large saloon

▲ *Grub first ... then sailing.*

▲ *Sea trials: Sam Bos surveys while the engines roar.*

ports that go underwater when she heels. His only comment: *I guess I will have to get used to looking through salty portholes in the harbor.*" In fairness to him, this curt, almost resigned statement concealed an abundance of thoughts and feelings. This was the beginning of the end; the last stage of an exhausting, expensive five-year program: His commissioning of this masterpiece was almost fulfilled; the yard he would miss visiting was already behind him; the "hole" in his life nearly filled; the melancholy of things completed sinking in. And there was frustration in his tone: Five years had passed and he was sailing a boat that wasn't yet his, still carried a Dutch flag, was commanded by the yard's captain, was insured by the yard's underwriters and still had no carpets, drapes, cushions, lamps or sofas. His emotions were no doubt buried under the weight of his own Utopian demands, under the weight of the incomplete achievement and an almost hopeless schedule to finish hundreds of items in time to get *Juliet* across the Atlantic to celebrate 217 years of America's independence – a perfectly appropriate debut for such a paradigm of independence.

Yet, it was entirely of his own doing, this drawn-out program, this obsession with detail, this quest for perfection. Each moment, therefore, was an eternity until this still-Dutch ketch was his to take away. He had left Vollenhove behind; now he just wanted to leave these coveralled men behind and go sailing. This was April 24, 1993; the signing of the protocol to turn over the ownership to him still lay twenty pressure-filled days in the future.

Those twenty days in Den Helder – with the *Vita Pugna*, dog and parrot (and a new chef) alongside – boomed with more activity, and inevitable minor flaws were revealed: some alarms rang for trivial reasons; the propeller pitch control needed a tweak; a minor hydraulic leak developed; a halyard toggle failed, and generator exhausts were found to be so efficient (as the yard had suspected) some water jacketing had to be removed. And the crow's nest was also removed several times for adjustment (between giddy trials by the owner's visiting friends). But most systems tested out perfectly. There was plenty of good, loud music from the stereos; nature provided warm and cold days to confirm

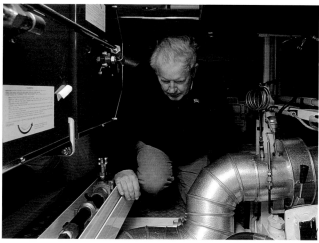

▲ *Wolter Huisman: the final inspection.*

the air-conditioning and heating; the Inmarsat "A" SatCom and radios proved out, and the dinghies seemed to hold their air.

The main anchoring system was also tested, in 20 meters of water. Erik van Hulst, pushbutton in hand, slowly lowered the 220-kilo CQR bower. The anchor whip slid the flukes clear of the hull before the shank tipped and the anchor headed for the bottom, followed by a good portion of the 140 meters of clinking 19-mm galvanized-steel chain. Van Hulst reversed the variable-speed Steen 23.50 capstan and the chain came up from the deep and returned, link-by-clinking-link, into its locker, followed by the anchor, which slid snugly into its hawsehole. So easily done.

But not every moment was that easy; one moment in particular unexpectedly tested the entire Huisman team's mettle to the fullest. Returning from routine trials, Mike Koppstein initiated bow and stern thrusters in preparation for docking. The Ricom computer started both 60-kW generators to power the thrusters, as it is supposed to. But moments later Koppstein found that the throttle and gearbox controls had ceased functioning; *Juliet* drifted powerless in a narrow, heavily used shipping canal. Apparently, too many consumers were drawing power and the Ricom, sensing an overload in the remaining 15-kW generator, had shut it down. The generator was quickly restarted, but the computer failed to follow up by instructing the air compressor to restart as well; without compressed air the throttle and gearbox were unreachable, except by manual backup in the engine room. Instead, while Koppstein calmly held *Juliet* in the wind, the engineer restarted the compressor and control was regained. Later, a reprogram of the computer and a bit of rewiring precluded this failure in future. The systems designers learned a great deal that day. That, after all, is what sea trials are all about.

Between trial days, carpenters, drapers and upholsterers with shears, knives, tape measures and sewing machines began to fill in settees, cover floors and curtain ports. Though they had to work around carpenter's tool boxes and avoid tripping over electricians' feet, they gradually added new color and sculptural form to every cozy mahogany corner. In the dark of the evenings, with the workers singing and relaxing on the hotel barge astern, the

▲ *The mate does his work …*

▲ ... *and the thrusters do theirs.*

owner would try out those corners, even in their various stages of incompletion. Some days, to escape the clash of workers, he flew off to London or Paris in search of oil paintings, table lamps or wall fixtures, and on his return he searched for the ideal spot to mount them. It was also during this period that a quiet, elfin man from Germany, Fritz Müller, came by to take measurements for the last bit of *Juliet*'s canvas work, the Bimini top, having already made the aft dodger, lee boards and covers for pedestals, wheels, hatches, capstan, fenders, deck tables, chairs, winches, dinghies, outboards, cushions, ironing board and interior furniture.

Also, in those last weeks in Den Helder, the protracted negotiations for *Juliet*'s insurance coverage were finally consummated. With the yard's policy soon to pass out of effect, at the official turnover, this was a critical moment that could not be delayed. Once a yacht goes off on the ocean and confronts heavy weather or just anchors tranquilly thousands of miles from the protection of home, she, her crew and guests face ever-present risks and dangers: Collision, accident, physical damage, bodily harm, illness, theft, vandalism and natural disaster lurk within every passage, beyond every tack or jibe. These can be costly experiences and it is essential that an owner have a clear, exhaustive mechanism for being fairly compensated in light of those risks, written into an incontrovertible insurance policy. The brokerage house that wrote *Juliet*'s insurance is Pantaenius, an old, established firm based in Hamburg, Germany, with a branch in Plymouth, England. Pantaenius is a dedicated specialist in marine insurance, with 25,000 racing and cruising yachts under its wing, most based in Europe but many cruising the world. In addition to handling those policies, and thousands of claims annually, Pantaenius has gone a major step further to serve clients by establishing a Marine Claims Service, a worldwide network of contacts to assist clients in swiftly getting replacements, repairs, haulout and recovery of stolen items (including their boats). In recent years Pantaenius has written an increasing number policies for large yachts, and insures most Royal Huisman yachts built since 1980 (this includes the first *Flyer*, whose April 1990 crushing in a Panama Canal accident was quickly resolved in her owner's favor).

In assessing risks and setting the premium for *Juliet*'s insurance Pantaenius had to typically consider the repute of the yard that built her, her machinery and navigation gear, the intricacy of her systems, her planned and unforeseen destinations and to a large extent the experience of her crew. Indeed, *Juliet*'s crew of six has enormous collective experience. Yet, during these trials they too were facing a monumental

challenge: to coalesce, to assume obligations and to learn to operate their new enigmatic charge. The captain, Herb Kiendl, familiarized himself with systems, navigation and taming of the beast. Paddy Lynch, the administrative guru, saw to every remaining detail in preparation for life offshore, from the finish of the interior to provisions and shipboard management. The Aussie mate, Ken Gray, spliced, whipped and leathered everything from rigging to chairbacks, and told long tales of the South Pacific. The Kiwi engineer, Steve Laing, donned blue Huisman coveralls and buried himself in his white-painted sepulchre, gaining conversational agility with "HAL," sorting through more than 65 volumes of manuals. The American deckhand, Mike Eudenbach, crawled into every nook and bilge to know where, why and how difficult to stow everything was. His countrywoman, Erika Arndt, the cook, quickly plunged into the microcosm of the galley and began immediately sending out superb grub. Together the crew also made the awful but not unexpected discovery that carpets and furniture need daily vacuuming, each morning about 150 linear meters of caprail and 103 square meters of deckhouse need the embrace of the chamois, and 206 square meters of teak decking often require the brush. The mate, in an off moment, equated *Juliet*'s *total* surface area — topsides and bottom included — to forty-seven 1932 Peugeot 201C sedans (recalling that Huisman painter Kees van Dokkemburg had rebuilt one), or fifty-one 1993 Volkswagen Golfs (honoring Pon Holdings, the conglomerate that among its many works leases clean Volkswagen Golfs to thousands of clients, including the Royal Huisman Shipyard).

Juliet's under-sail trials, also set by protocol, took place under a wide range of wind conditions, fortuitously giving Robbie Doyle, Herman Slot, Ron Holland, Wolter and the owner, satisfying answers to all the questions about her performance. One hazy day, despite her size and full load, she close-reached at four knots in no more than four knots of shear-ridden breeze (measured at her masthead, 160 feet above a shimmering sea). On another, breezier, day with some VIPs aboard, she was assaulted by 35 to 40 knots and proved that her reefed Doyle sails retained their shape, that she remained balanced and that her Rondal furlers and winches made easy work of the exceptional pressures put upon them. On that day — while all sheets were bar-taut, the rig was loaded to the maximum and seas were breaking over the bow — a visitor could slip into the saloon and *feel* the silence below. At one hushed moment, with the rail awash and the North Sea rushing by the leeward saloon ports in great scintil-

◄ *Crow's nest, used and observed.*

▲ *Anchor tests always attract a crowd.*

▲ *Rondal's chief rigger, Herman Slot, at home aloft.*

lating green swirls, one could listen heedfully for some slight groaning or creaking – *any* noise – yet discern only one sound: the faint, rhythmic scraping of books on the saloon shelves as they tipped to and fro with the tumbling sea. It was at that very moment that Ron Holland, subdued perhaps by the wonder of his own creation, asked a guest rhetorically: "She feels solid, doesn't she?"

On yet another day, in moderate breezes, her trial watchers were momentarily distracted by the presence of Crown Prince Willem Alexander, son of beloved Queen Beatrix, a descendant of Prince William of Orange and next in line for Holland's honored leadership. Alex, as he insisted he be called, took the helm, felt its power and pronounced *Juliet* worthy. But if anyone were to discover the best feelings about *Juliet*, it would have been the day the sun shone brightly and the breeze was fresh but not hard. In the late morning it blew at about 15 knots. Sails were unfurled and trimmed, and a number of guests who had an unquenchable desire to "take the conn," including ecstatic Huisman board members, were overjoyed to steer her at 12 to 14 knots. Then the wind came up for a glistening hour to a steady 22 knots. The crew trimmed to an apparent wind angle of 35 degrees, the instruments showed an apparent wind speed of 35 knots and under full sail *Juliet* put her head down to the buffeting waves and her shoulder to the rolling seas. She heeled 18 degrees and held steady; her bow sent spume into the air; her foredeck turned the lustrous dark color of sea-drenched teak. Wolter took the helm. To Wolter Huisman, whose love and respect for the sea make him always a humble man, the moment was quietly satisfying. The owner took the helm. For him, five years of tensions were suddenly unleashed, if only temporarily, funnelled into an overdue smile that for the first time reached his eyes, an indication of a genuine sense of achievement, if not yet bliss.

Then a visiting writer took the helm. Like Wolter and the owner, he heard the shouts of guests gathered at the speedometer, egging him on as the big numbers flashed: "14," "15," then "16." Settling into "the groove," the writer found sailing this machine nothing less than exhilarating. The helm seat was just right; he could see bow, sails and the oncoming sea. The water rushed by, close under him in the foamy green trough, giving him a sense of speed that no mere number could give. The helm was balanced perfectly: wind and sea fed subtle messages through the rudder, the hydraulic rams and wheel, and if he concentrated on reading those messages he could keep her charging at better than 16 knots, with one hand on the wheel. And she responded to the wheel; its slightest movement was met by a slight swing of her bow, more than 100 feet away; otherwise she plunged powerfully forward as if on rails, proof of Ron Holland's superb architecture. Flying along, this creature of nearly 570,000 pounds drew energy from the wind and returned the energy to the sea whence it came, unrelentingly pushing 9,000 cubic feet of water out of her way, parting the incompressible sea.

Sailing her at 16.5 knots, the writer recalled every moment in which he had been in perfect tune with a graceful craft under sail. What more could be asked of life than to experience such kinetic, nature-driven energy, to sail a 570,000-pound hull at 16 knots? This is why men commission large sailing yachts, and why writers write about them. The only mistake a writer could have made that magic day was not to have gone up in the crow's nest to view the rig, the wake, the blue sky, the white-capped sea and curvature of the Earth. The writer made that mistake: So long as the breeze held fresh and cool in his face, so long as the water streamed by under him at 16 knots, so long as the Earth would remain curved to be viewed another day, he refused to relinquish the wheel. Happy he is that he did, before this beauty got away.

• • •

Twenty years a dream, five a process, this commissioned creation had come miraculously together: the alloy, systems and wood; the pumps, rig and cake mixer. But it had not been easy in those final anxious days. Laying alongside her 180-foot barge like an oversize baby whale clinging desperately to her mother, *Juliet* had been assembled, opened up and reassembled several times, and at times there was hardly room for workers to touch up paint, install handrails, check the gyrocompass or lay the last carpet. Yet, by the 14th of May, only a few stragglers and the crew remained to wipe down the varnish, snap in the overheads and fluff up the pillows. Fuel, water, food, dinnerware, wine, bedding and paperback books were stowed. Bongos, a guitar, a new Van Morrison CD, a mountain of personal gear and, finally, the golf clubs were tucked away. The inflatables were in davits or lashed on deck, the clinker tucked in the lazarette.

The turnover to her new owner of a Royal Huisman yacht is a treasured moment for the yard's 200 employees. While they work on a yacht they focus so diligently on the task for which they are trained, they may never have a sense of the yacht's totality: Day after day welders see only gray metal and blue light, joiners only wood, and painters just a fog of spray. Yet every one of them wants to view that totality when the boat emerges, to see how their task dovetails with all the others – it is

◄ *Wolter Huisman, Ron Holland.*

▲ *After a hard day's trials, reaching for home.*

the essence of their teamwork, their brotherhood. Every worker – including the women and men of the Huisman office staff – also wants (and surely deserves) to celebrate the entire team's triumph at a party, and if possible to go for a test sail. So on Saturday, May 15, the yard and the owner obliged them all with an open-house to beat all open houses. More than 400 guests were bused to Den Helder. Leaving their coveralls at home, they boarded a triple-decked excursion boat, with elegantly set tables, bars, a bandstand and bouquets of gorgeous Dutch flowers. Only 40 could go for a sail, in deference to safety, and they were previously selected by drawing lots. They climbed aboard and *Juliet* headed out of the harbor followed by the party boat. Outside, while captain Kiendl and his crew tacked and jibed her in long lazy reaches to show off her shape and speed, those in the party boat pointed at her with pride, took photos and spoke animatedly to their spouses and companions of *Juliet*'s great dimensions and rare qualities – of the unique place she occupies in their hearts. Each saw that totality in his or her own way.

When the boats returned to the harbor, the celebration continued with toasts, a sprawling buffet, music and dancing. Then over coffee and dessert Wolter gave a brief testimonial expressing his own joy of achievement and reminding his team that it had been well worth enduring the owner's unrelenting demands, particularly as it inspired such a superior result. The owner thanked Wolter and his team for their talent and perseverance. Then he recalled his youth, his early sailing adventures, his attempt to build an inexpensive ferrocement boat (because that was all he could afford) and the nights he was awakened by police as he slept in his caravan. "With my new van," he concluded, pointing to *Juliet*, "I don't have to worry about the police; I can get a good night's sleep." That Saturday night, after the party ended, *everyone* had a good night's sleep.

On Monday, May 17, 1993, with the sea trials complete, the protocol of ownership was signed and the last check was handed over. In place of the Dutch flag *Juliet* had carried on her stern for six weeks, there now fluttered a big "Red Duster," symbol of the ownership transfer. On that same Monday, the workers of the Royal Huisman Shipyard BV went back to work, at their carpenter's benches, welding machines, drafting boards, computers and desks, many wearing blue coveralls again. The joiners went on installing the cherry-panelled interior in *Borkumriff*, again seeing only wood; the welders went on completing *Saudade*'s superstructure, facing only gray metal and blue light once more; the draftsmen and computer designers concentrated on Henry Scheel's spider web of hull lines, as they had done before. The gap left by *Juliet*'s departure was filled.

Work and life in Vollenhove went on as before.

▲ *This is why men commission great yachts …*

▲ *... and why writers and photographers document them.*

"The wind is rising ... we must attempt to live." –
Paul Valery

to Den Helder, farewell to Holland. The crew, the owner and a few close friends from various warm corners of his life huddled on deck, taking last-minute videos and photos. Erik van Hulst, Mike Koppstein and his wife Cathy came aboard to offer experienced

hands and calm assistance for the maiden voyage. And a young Huisman painter, Andre Bakker, joined the crew for his first offshore sail, his first trip to America.

Wolter, wearing his signature gray slacks, navy blazer, striped tie and blue sailing coat, and commercial director Evert van Dishoeck, a fine sailor in his own right, stood by on the barge to assist. A few quick hugs and kisses had to suffice for this emotional climax to five years of partnership. Wolter and Evert handed lines to the crew as Herb Kiendl gently tilted two joysticks to port: 170 horsepower of thrusters churned up the water to starboard and slowly pushed *Juliet* into the fairway. Kiendl turned her around, signalled the bridge operator he was coming through for the last

▲ Juliet, *off Camden, Maine, with all her toys deployed.*

▲ *The crew: Herb, Steve, Paddy, Erika, Ken and Mike.*

time, put the throttle in forward and 840 more horses drove her through the bridge, to the outer harbor, toward the sea.

After launching nearly 160 aluminum boats in fewer than 30 years, Wolter Huisman, in a thoughtful mood, once said of such pivotal moments in his life: "It's always nice to see a new baby go. Yes, a little bit of pressure is off – not that there is always so much pressure. But I live so long with each boat, when it finally leaves the dock, I can give it to the owner…. It's not so hard." It is possible, however, that Wolter Huisman found giving *Juliet* away a bit harder than most. She was his largest, and surely his most accomplished "baby" to date; he had lived with her far longer than any boat in his half-century of building them; he and his workers had put more of themselves into her than any yacht that preceded her.

Wolter's moist eyes told the story of just how hard it was to see her off, even though he would see her again, as he said, "on the other side." As *Juliet* headed for the bridge, he and Van Dishoeck waved, then together they jumped into Wolter's car and drove to the mouth of Den Helder's harbor, to Land's End, a sandy, desolate point overlooking the sea. A silvery mist had set in, softening everything in view, even the rumbling, hard-edged Texel ferry. Wolter parked the car and turned the high beams on as a last signal of connection to *Juliet* – as though he hoped that the beams, defying all cosmological principle, could hold her forever in their grip and his, a sort of last-ditch semaphore of pride mixed with resignation. As she motored farther out over the flat sea she was eventually swallowed in the haze, as if falling into a black hole; soon the connection between the headlights and the faint light reflected from her brilliant white hull weakened and faded.

The departure was done.

• ● •

Juliet entered the North Sea shipping lanes and turned southwest to the Straits of Dover and to England. As she neared the white cliffs, her engineer transmitted a cryptic fax back to the shipyard: *No alarms yet*. Its meaning, however, was crystal clear in Vollenhove: *The Ricom is behaving*. On May 24, *Juliet* was filled with more than 20 metric tons of fuel and the gear of 14 people

▲ *The 12-foot clinker-built in the 14-foot hold.*

and she headed southwest, to the Channel Islands, then toward the sunset, toward the Azores. But off the Bay of Biscay – whose name is synonymous with miserable weather – she was hit by miserable weather: her first trial by the sea's special brand of fire. Though she handled the high winds and heavy seas with aplomb, as a world cruiser must, a few inexperienced guests did not take kindly to the motion and Kiendl detoured *Juliet* to Vigo, on Spain's northwest corner, to favor them with solid footing. Continuing on June 6, the group traversed the 950 nautical miles to Faial, in the Azores, where they water skied, searched ashore for tender Portuguese steak and rough red wine and enjoyed the salubrious salt air. And there, as *Juliet* lay along the seawall that forms Horta's inviolate harbor – as ancient tradition inescapably demands – Andre Bakker painted a "Huisman-quality" logo and illustration, to assure *Juliet*'s continued safe voyaging.

Then Kiendl set his initial great-circle course of 269^0 True to Bermuda, and the wind obliged by piping up again. For a time *Juliet* was driven by 30 to 40 knot squalls on her quarter. But all hands knew her by now, and had a better idea of how to answer the power of the storm with sail trim and helm. They stood their watches in confident, friendly groups. During one chilly, particularly grim squall, with heavy pelting rain flattening the roiled sea, she surged to 19.4 knots, her highest speed yet, which inspired the cook to prepare a seaworthy stick-to-the-ribs supper of spaghettini, fresh-ground parmigian, pea pods, chicken strips and vinaigrette salad, just one majestic meal among many. (As the great observer of sailors and the sea, Boris Lauer-Leonardi, wrote: "… only a good cook can give a ship the sound foundation on which the skipper can build a happy cruise.")

And so this happy cruise continued, with companions sharing work and enlightenment, under full or shortened sail, sometimes under power, as *Juliet* plunged westward, covering the 1,800 nautical miles from Horta to Bermuda in seven days, two hours, averaging an effortless 10.5 knots. From Bermuda, it was a short hop to Newport and *Juliet*'s stunning debut before the eyes of knowing American sailors and gaping American tourists. It was approaching the Independence Day weekend, a time for outdoor

▲ *Andre Bakker in Horta: Once a painter, always a painter.*

▲ Juliet *and her classic kin in the "Nantucket Bucket Race."*

celebration, a time for fireworks. First, however, it was a time, briefly, for reality: the initial installment of one contract year of warranty work, a standard yard procedure.

Jan Bokxem, who can be as honest as he is talented, has said: "When a boat leaves us I always wave goodbye proudly," adding with a wry smile, "then I hope that I don't hear from them for a year." But machinery, materials and builders, like life, are imperfect. Which is why Mike Koppstein came down from his office in Ogunquit, Maine, and Bert Tromp, a Huisman troubleshooter, flew in from Amsterdam to iron out problems that had developed

during the crossing. Then *Juliet* – with only ten months left in her warranty period, but perhaps never to be truly finished – went off to sail the world. First to Martha's Vineyard for July 4th fireworks, then on to Nantucket and Maine. In the autumn she would head south to the Caribbean; the following spring she would head west again, easily transiting the wide Panama Canal (unlike the narrow Dutch canals of her birth), and from there she would sail anywhere her owner chose: into many quiet bays (so long as they offered depth enough for her 15-foot keel), to many remote islands (so long as the wind held free or the fuel held up), over new horizons

rightly and the owner's desire remained undiminished).

In sailing to her unknown, unknowable destiny, this yacht, this commissioned masterpiece named *Juliet*, will witness many more fireworks displays, whether for July 4th in American waters, Bastille Day in French, Midsummer's Night in Scandinavia or New Year's Eve anywhere. We do not know if the Emperor Justinian set off fireworks when one of his 10,000 laborers laid the final brick in the dome of *Hagia Sophia*; it is certain that the French did set off fireworks when the *Eiffel Tower* was opened to the world in

as *Juliet* must always honor the workers whose long days and skilled hands completed them. The idea of such honor and such celebration echoes through the centuries to this day. That is why our own 20th-Century entrepreneur, *Juliet*'s owner, reflecting back on his five-year love affair with Vollenhove and with the workers of the Royal Huisman Shipyard BV, used these words to sum up his sometimes exhausting, always exhilarating experience:

"So many men.... So much caring."

* * *

▲ *The masterpiece created....*

The authors are indebted to the following companies and institutions who helped us document *Juliet*'s creation and enabled us to produce this unique book.

AGA Gas BV
Distelweg 90
1031 HH Amsterdam
The Netherlands

Coopers & Lybrand
Burg van Royensingel 2
8011 CS Zwolle
The Netherlands

Pon Holdings BV
Huis "De Salentein"
Putterstraatweg 5
3862 RA Nijkerk
The Netherlands

Awlgrip NV
Bouwelven 1
Industriezone Klein Gent
2280 Grobbendonk
Belgium

Jens Cornelsen
Yacht Consultant
Jungfernstieg 11
2208 Glückstadt
Germany

Ron Holland Design
PO Box 23,
Kinsale,
County Cork
Ireland

Pieter Beeldsnijder
Voorhaven 20 - 22
1135 BR Edam
The Netherlands

Doyle Sailmakers
89 Front Street
Marblehead
Massachusetts 01945
USA

Hoogovens
Aluminium
Walzprodukte
GmbH
Carl-Spaeter Strasse 10
5400 Koblenz
Germany

BTICINO s.p.a.
Corso Porta Vittoria 9
20122 Milano
Italy

Franken BV
Balendijk 13
3900 Lommel
Belgium

Houtbedrijf Van Hout BV
Wanroyseweg 2 - 6
5451 HA Mill
The Netherlands

Brookes & Gatehouse Ltd
Bath Road
Lymington
Hampshire SO41 9YP
England

Furuno Electric Co. Ltd
9-52, Ashihara-cho
Nishinimiya 662
Japan

Royal Huisman
Shipyard BV
Flevoweg 1
8325 PA Vollenhove
The Netherlands

Centraalstaal BV
Euvelgunnerweg 25
9700 AE Groningen
The Netherlands

Gemeente Brederwiede
Groenestraat 24
8325 AX Vollenhove
The Netherlands

Cito Benelux BV
Hengelder 56
6902 PA Zevenaar
The Netherlands

Geo. Gleistein & Sohn
GmbH
Heidlerchenstr. 7
2820 Bremen 71
Germany

Hundested
motor-& propeller
fabrik a/s
Skansevej 1 - 9
3390 Hundested
Denmark

Condaria '87 SRL
Via Fogazzaro, 16
20092 Cinisello Balsamo
Milano
Italy

Hasco Lakfabrieken
Scheepmakershaven 11
2871 CE Schoonhoven
The Netherlands

Imco Holland BV
Giessenweg 25
3044 AK Rotterdam
The Netherlands

Gideonweg 5/5
9723 BM Groningen
The Netherlands

Centrum Groningen BV
Euvelgunnerweg 25
9723 CV Groningen
The Netherlands

Croeselaan 163
3521 BL Utrecht
The Netherlands

MTU
Motoren- und
Turbinen-Union
Friedrichshafen GmbH
Olgastraße 75
7990 Friedrichshafen 1
Germany

Pantaenius Yacht
Insurance Brokers
Cremon 32
2000 Hamburg 1
Germany

Sea Recovery
Corporation
13650 Cimarron Avenue
Gardena, Ca. 90249
U. S. A.

Auto- und Bootssattlerei
Müller GmbH
Mühlenweg 34
4630 Bochum 1
Germany

Riggarna
Unit 3, Somerford
Business Park
Wilverley Road
Christchurch
Dorset, BH23 3RU
England

Speck Pompen
Nederland BV
Lorentzstraat 1
6902 PZ Zevenaar
The Netherlands

ING Bank
De Amsterdamse Poort
Bijlmerplein 888
1102 MG Amsterdam
The Netherlands

Rondal BV
De Weyert 30
8325 EM Vollenhove
Holland

Steen Deck Machinery
Maschinenfabrik/
Engineeringworks
K. Christian Steen GmbH
Carl-Zeiss-Strasse 4
2200 Elmshorn
Germany

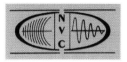
Noise & Vibration
Consultancy
Noordhoek 37
3351 LD Papendrecht
The Netherlands

Woodindustry
Bros Van Rozendaal BV
Spoorlaan 12
5481 SK Schijndel
The Netherlands

Victron Energie BV
Keienbergweg 24
1101 GB Amsterdam
The Netherlands

... and last, but by no means least:

Atsa batterijen BV
Energieweg 105
3641 RT Mijdrecht
The Netherlands

Bennex Holland BV
Edisonweg 10
3208 KB Spijkenisse
The Netherlands

Bruynzeel Multipanel BV
Pieter Ghijssenlaan 20
1506 PV Zaandam
The Netherlands

Cleton Insulation BV
Industriestr. 26
7891 AA Klazienaveen
The Netherlands

Ehringa Media
Audiovisuele Techniek
Energieweg 7
9743 AN Groningen
The Netherlands

Emmeloordse Glashandel
Korte Achterzijde 10
8300 AK Emmeloord
The Netherlands

Exalto BV
Nijverheidsstraat 12-14
3371 XE Hardinxveld
The Netherlands

Heinemann Electrics
c/o Bredant
Grote Spie 355
4819 CW Breda
The Netherlands

A.G.J. Hendriks Interieurs
Schapenmeent 214-215
1357 GV Almere-Haven
The Netherlands

Rollins Hudig Hall
Grote Bickersstraat 74
1013 KS Amsterdam
The Netherlands

Phoenix Contact BV
Hengelder 56
6902 PA Zevenaar
The Netherlands

v. Rietschoten & Houwens
Technology BV
Industrieweg 30
3361 HJ Sliedrecht
The Netherlands

Rittal BV
Hengelder 56
6902 PA Zevenaar
The Netherlands